SHOW & TELL

SHOW & TELL

HOW EVERYBODY CAN MAKE EXTRAORDINARY PRESENTATIONS

DAN ROAM

PORTFOLIO / PENGUIN

PORTFOLIO / PENGUIN
Published by the Penguin Group
Penguin Group (USA) LLC
375 Hudson Street
New York, New York 10014

USA | Canada | UK | Ireland | Australia | New Zealand | India | South Africa | China
penguin.com
A Penguin Random House Company

First published by Portfolio / Penguin, a member of Penguin Group (USA) LLC, 2014

Illustration credits
AAA Pathways: Pages 90–107
© 2013, Spectrum Health. All rights reserved: Pages 118–133
iStockphoto: Pages 215, 216, 218, 219

ISBN 978-1-59184-685-7

Printed in the United States of America
10 9 8 7 6 5 4 3 2 1

Set in Verlag
Designed by Daniel Lagin

For Isabelle, Sophie, and Celeste
(And you too, Ms. Puma)

How to
make an
extraordinary
presentation:

①

Tell the
Truth.

② Tell it with a Story.

③ Tell the story with pictures.

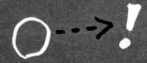

CONTENTS

THESE TOOLS WILL HELP US ALONG THE WAY

1. A **pyramid** to help with truth

2. An **outline** to help with stories

3. A **pie** to help with the pictures

ONE SIMPLE THOUGHT

If I tell you the truth, I tell it with a story, and if I tell that story with pictures, I can keep you glued to your seat. **Let me show you how.**

SHOW & TELL

CHAPTER 1
THE THREE RULES

As presenters, our goal is simple:
To help others see what we see.

To do this, we:
entertain
educate
persuade
motivate
and ultimately
change
our audience.

In other words, we create and deliver a **report**, **explanation**, **pitch**, or **story** so captivating that our audience *wants* to see things the way we do.

That sounds pretty simple.

It should be easy.

But it's not.

So here's the question: If presenting is so easy, why is it so hard?

Because we forget to *show* and *tell*.

THE THREE RULES OF SHOW AND TELL:

1. Lead with the truth and the **heart** will follow.

2. Lead with a story and **understanding** will follow.

3. Lead with the eye and the **mind** will follow.

1. Truth → Heart

When we tell the truth in a presentation, three good things happen: We connect with our audience, we become passionate, and we find self-confidence.

2. Story → Understanding

When we tell a story in a presentation, three great things happen: We make complex concepts clear, we make ideas unforgettable, and we include everyone.

3. Eye → Mind

When we tell a story with pictures in a presentation, extraordinary things happen: People see exactly what we mean, we captivate our audience's mind, and we banish boredom.

CHAPTER 2
RULE 1:
TELL THE TRUTH

Lead with the truth
and the heart will follow.

It was one of the best speeches I ever heard,
because it was truth rather than horsesh#t.

—**STEPHEN KING**

If you tell the truth, you don't have to remember anything.

—**MARK TWAIN**

What is an extraordinary presentation?
One that changes people.
What makes people change?
The truth.

There is no faster way to establish trust with our audience than to tell the truth.

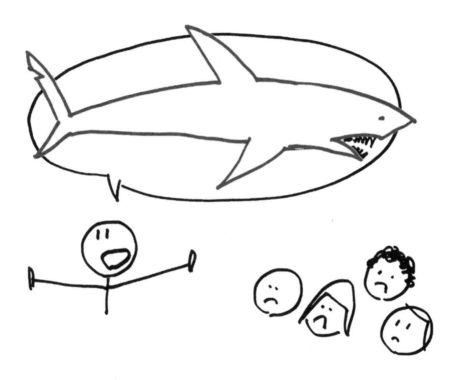

There is no faster way to lose our audience than to B.S.

That said, there is more than one kind of truth.

Our **HEAD** says:
"I think this is true."
(Intellectual truth)

Our **HEART** says:
"I believe this is true."
(Emotional truth)

Our **DATA** say:
"The facts tell me this is true."
(Factual truth)

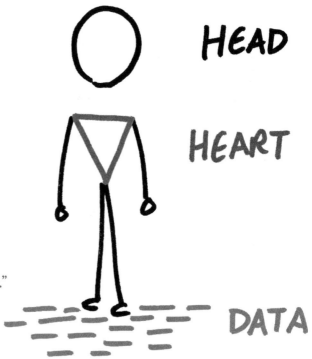

HEAD

HEART

DATA

All three truths live in us all the time.
For example, we might look at this and say:

"*The glass is half _____ .*"

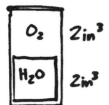

The **DATA** tell me:
Volume of O_2 = 2 in³
Volume of H_2O = 2 in³

My **HEAD** knows:
A half-full glass is a source of hope.
A half-empty glass is a source of despair.

My **HEART** believes:
The glass is half full!

Which one of these truths is correct?
They all are.

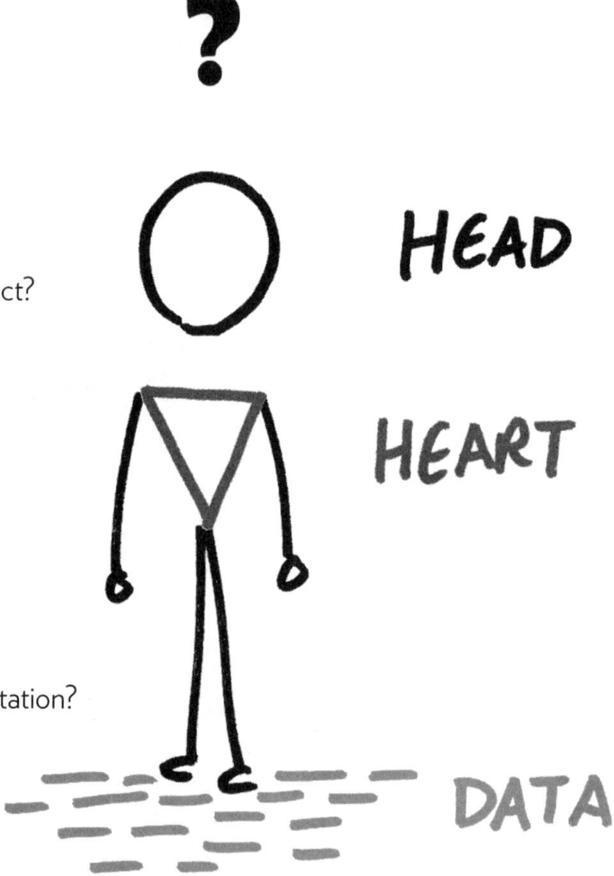

? HEAD

HEART

Which one makes a better presentation?
That depends.

DATA

NOT ALL OF THESE TRUTHS ARE EQUAL.

Things we **BELIEVE** outrank things we **KNOW**.
And both outrank "**JUST THE FACTS.**"

A good presentation shares new data.
A great presentation changes what we know.
An extraordinary presentation changes what we believe.

As a presenter, the first question we need to ask ourselves is:

For this topic, for this audience, and for myself, which truth should I tell?

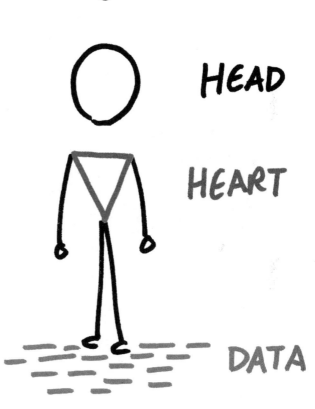

There is a simple way to answer that question.
Let's call it

"The Bucket Rule."

ALL PRESENTATIONS ARE COMPOSED OF JUST THREE ELEMENTS.

Our Idea

Us

Our Audience

This is the idea, concept, lesson, tool, or rule we want to share.

This is us, and we've got something to share.

This is our audience; these are the people we want to share our idea with.

These are our three buckets.
Our job is to line them up:

MY
IDEA

MY
SELF

MY
AUDIENCE

Next, we fill them up with our truths:

Thoughts, impressions, data, anecdotes, ideas, concerns . . .

My goals, hopes, beliefs, worries, insights . . .

Demographics, experience, abilities, skills, hidden agendas, aspirations, unknowns . . .

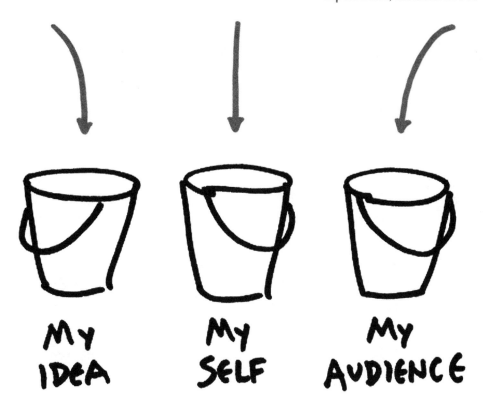

MY IDEA

MY SELF

MY AUDIENCE

BUCKET 1 = MY IDEA

BUCKET 2 = MY SELF

My BELIEF
My MESSAGE
My CONCEPT

My PRODUCT
My LESSON
My DISCOVERY

Quiet

Hilarious   Ha ha

Serious

Loud

Emotional

Who am I?

If I had all the freedom in the world to say exactly what I want, **What would I really want to say?**

Who am I really (or who do I most want to be) when I share this idea? Am I happy to share it or sad? Am I confident or unsure? Am I a believer or a skeptic? **What do I most want my audience to remember about me?**

BUCKET 3 = MY AUDIENCE

Who are they?

Who are the people on the other side of my idea?
What makes them tick? What needs do they have?
If my presentation could change them in just one way, what would that change be?

For example, imagine we wanted to pitch our new social media app to a venture capitalist. Here's how we would organize our buckets:

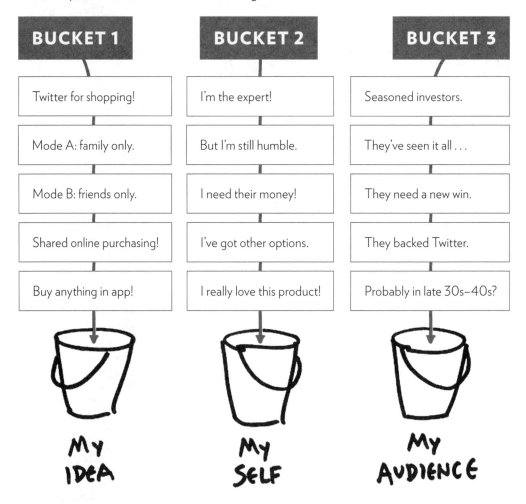

BUCKET 1	BUCKET 2	BUCKET 3
Twitter for shopping!	I'm the expert!	Seasoned investors.
Mode A: family only.	But I'm still humble.	They've seen it all . . .
Mode B: friends only.	I need their money!	They need a new win.
Shared online purchasing!	I've got other options.	They backed Twitter.
Buy anything in app!	I really love this product!	Probably in late 30s–40s?

MY IDEA

MY SELF

MY AUDIENCE

FROM THESE QUICK THOUGHTS, OUR PRESENTATION BEGINS TO TAKE SHAPE.

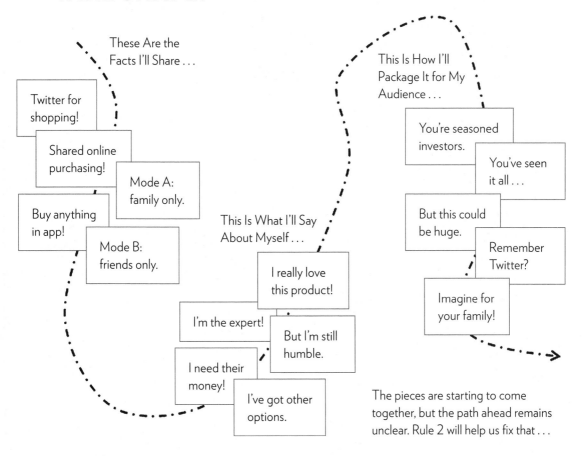

These Are the Facts I'll Share . . .

Twitter for shopping!

Shared online purchasing!

Buy anything in app!

Mode A: family only.

Mode B: friends only.

This Is What I'll Say About Myself . . .

I really love this product!

I'm the expert!

But I'm still humble.

I need their money!

I've got other options.

This Is How I'll Package It for My Audience . . .

You're seasoned investors.

You've seen it all . . .

But this could be huge.

Remember Twitter?

Imagine for your family!

The pieces are starting to come together, but the path ahead remains unclear. Rule 2 will help us fix that . . .

To summarize, *filling the buckets with truth* helps us to:

Pull together the pieces of our idea.
Have confidence in ourselves.
Get to know our audience.

Now it's time to craft our story.

Ready

CHAPTER 3

RULE 2: TELL IT WITH A STORY

LEAD WITH A STORY AND UNDERSTANDING WILL FOLLOW.

I have the "thing" worked out—the trick or the surprise or the pivotal fact. Then I just start somewhere and let the story work itself out.

—LEE CHILD

There have been great societies that did not use the wheel, but there have been no societies that did not tell stories.

—URSULA K. LE GUIN

THERE ARE ALL KINDS OF PRESENTATIONS.

Presentations that change the audience's INFORMATION.

Presentations that change the audience's ABILITIES.

Presentations that change the audience's ACTIONS.

Presentations that change the audience's BELIEFS.

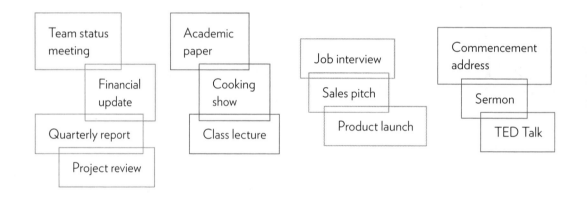

Team status meeting

Financial update

Quarterly report

Project review

Academic paper

Cooking show

Class lecture

Job interview

Sales pitch

Product launch

Commencement address

Sermon

TED Talk

An **ESPN** sportscast is nothing like a **Rachael Ray** cooking show, which is nothing like an **Apple** keynote, which is nothing like a **TED Talk**, yet all are wildly success-ful presentations.

How does that happen?

SUCCESSFUL PRESENTATIONS ARE BUILT ON CLEAR STORYLINES.

A good presentation always has a clear storyline.

It is not endless.

It is not confusing.

It is not random.

A STORYLINE IS THE BACKBONE OF ANY PRESENTATION. WHY?

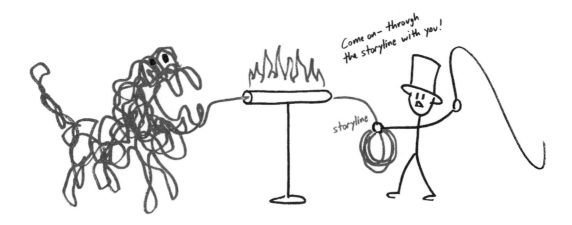

Clear storylines are our best defense against confusion. They force complexity into submission long enough to be tamed.

100% of all presentations can be made with just **four storylines**:

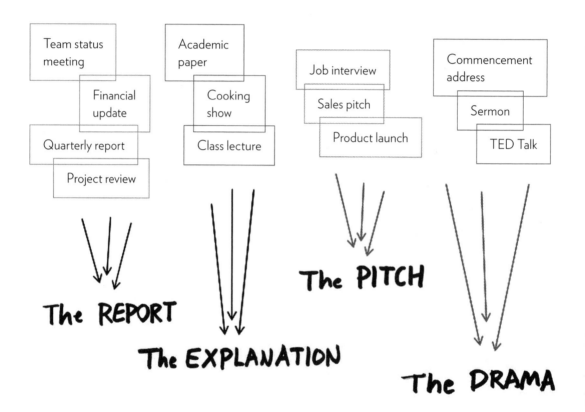

The **four storylines** look like this:

The REPORT

| Conveys the facts. |

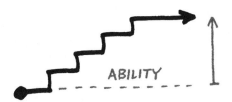

The EXPLANATION

| Teaches new insights or abilities. |

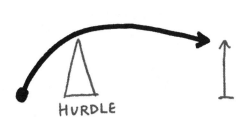

The PITCH

| Recommends a new action or solution. |

The DRAMA

| Inspires a new belief or way of looking at the world. |

Before we explore each in detail, here are the essentials:

The REPORT

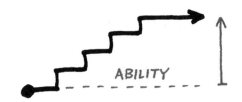

The EXPLANATION

THE **REPORT** BRINGS DATA TO LIFE.

With a report, we change our audience's INFORMATION. A good report delivers the facts. A great report makes the facts insightful and memorable.

THE **EXPLANATION** SHOWS US HOW.

With an explanation, we change our audience's KNOWLEDGE or ABILITY. A good explanation takes our audience to a new level. A great explanation makes it effortless.

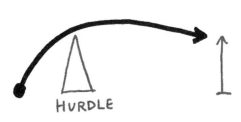

HURDLE

The PITCH

HAPPINESS

The DRAMA

THE PITCH GETS US OVER THE HURDLE.

With a pitch, we change our audience's **ACTIONS**.
A good pitch gives our audience a solution to a problem. A great pitch makes that solution undeniable.

THE DRAMA BREAKS OUR HEART, THEN MENDS IT.

With a drama, we change our audience's **BELIEFS**.
A good drama makes us feel someone's struggle. A great drama makes us feel the struggle is our own.

Each storyline is different, but they have two things in common:

1. **They have a beginning and an end.** One reason many presentations fail is because they don't go anywhere. **Good presentations always MOVE ALONG.**
2. **The end point is always higher than the beginning point.** Another reason presentations fail is because they don't trigger any change. **Good presentations always move UP.**

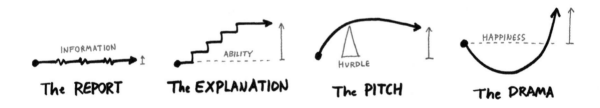

The REPORT   The EXPLANATION   The PITCH   The DRAMA

In other words, an extraordinary presentation begins with knowing **how far** and **how high** we want to take our audience.

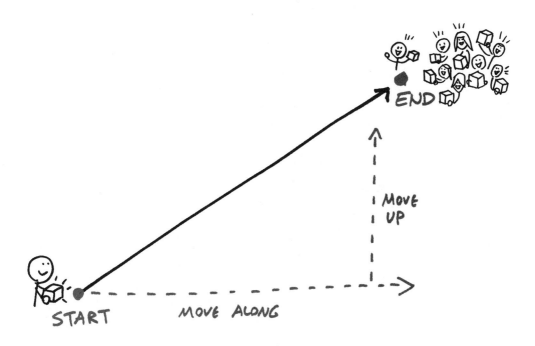

There are really only four ways we can **move** our audience:

1. We change their **information**.

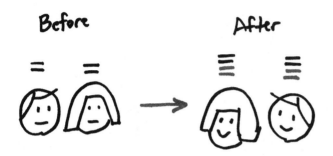

We add new data to something they already know.

2. We change their **knowledge or ability**.

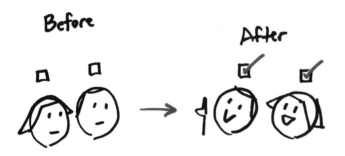

We share new insights or show them how to do something useful.

3. We change their actions.

We persuade them to do, use, try, or buy something new.

4. We change their beliefs.

We inspire them to understand something new about themselves and the world.

To pick the right storyline, all we need to do is answer the following question:

"After we've finished presenting, how do we want our audience to be **different** from when we started?"

How we answer that question tells us which storyline to use.

In other words, the **change** we want our audience to experience will determine which **storyline** we choose.

All storylines share the same components.

A storyline is like a living, breathing creature that moves our idea from beginning to end.

It has both a spine ------ that drives the presentation forward and supporting anecdotes ||||| that provide detail and color.

In management consultingese, this is called **"horizontal-vertical storytelling."**

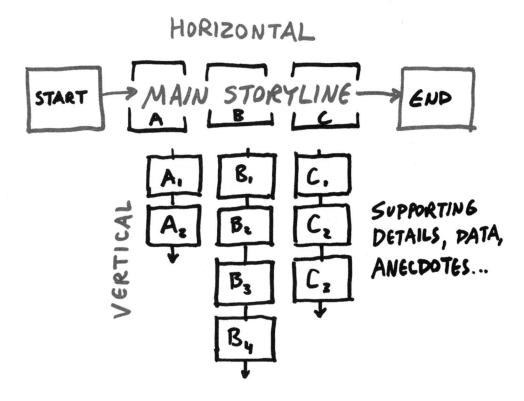

I prefer a livelier name:

Our storyline is our
Presentation's **U**nderlying **M**essage **A**rchitecture.

"PUMA"

The **PUMA** looks like this:

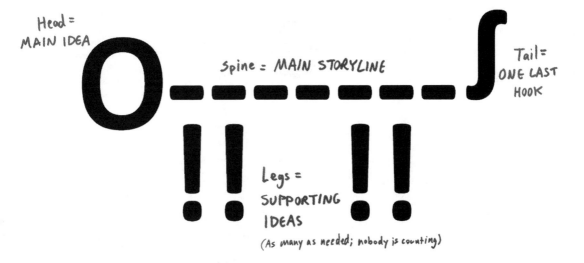

Head =
MAIN IDEA

Spine = MAIN STORYLINE

Tail =
ONE LAST
HOOK

Legs =
SUPPORTING
IDEAS

(As many as needed; nobody is counting)

Think of the **PUMA** as the shape of our storyline: We start with the main idea, we build a spine from the main storyline, we support the spine with details, and we end with a (last) final hook.

He
wasn't
kidding.

The **PUMA** gives us a good way to build* our presentation.

1. We begin with a summary
   of our main idea.

2. Then we block out the
   spine with our storyline.

*We usually CREATE our PUMA from head to tail, but we might not present it that way. We'll talk more about this later in this section.

3. We add in our supporting
   materials as the legs.

4. We conclude with a swish
   of the tail.

For example, here is a **PUMA** outline of a classic story:

Boy meets girl

This is the tale of a typical Hollywood romance . . .

There is a boy. He meets a girl.

The boy loses the girl.

The boy gets the girl back.

The girl runs off with the assistant.

The boy is carefree.

The girl is lovely.

The boy is smitten.

Mr. Evil arrives.

Mr. Evil steals the girl away!

The boy is devastated.

The boy hires an assistant.

The assistant traps Mr. Evil.

The boy saves the girl!

The **PUMA** also helps us build a more prosaic story:

Our sales team status update

Our team has recovered from a bad year.

The past year was hard.

The market tanked.

Everyone suffered.

We thought it was over.

Last quarter looked pretty good.

The market stabilized.

We doubled down on the basics.

Sales returned to precrash levels.

Next quarter looks awesome!

New markets are opening.

We're ahead of the curve.

We're hiring top talent again.

Now's the time to launch our new product!

In this book we will meet four **PUMA**s: one for each of the four storylines.

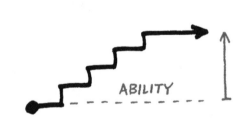

INFORMATION

The resting PUMA is the **report**.

The REPORT

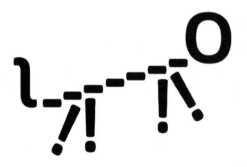

The climbing PUMA is the **explanation**.

ABILITY

The EXPLANATION

The pouncing PUMA is the **pitch**.

The PITCH

HURDLE

The leaping PUMA is the **drama**.

The DRAMA

HAPPINESS

This I've got to see...

(Our PUMA rests.)

The report presents the data.
With a report, we change our audience's information.

INFORMATION

The REPORT

A SO-SO REPORT DELIVERS THE DATA.

Reports are the most frequent presentations we make.

They are also the most likely to fail.

Why? Because most reports *by design* tell us what we already know, then add a few things we don't. They are typically written to eliminate any surprise or drama.

That's not a very memorable or actionable proposition.

A GOOD REPORT BRINGS DATA TO LIFE.

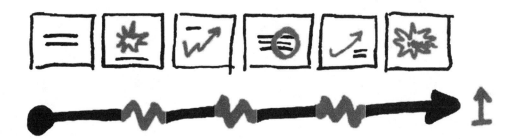

When we do a report right, we deliver more than just the facts; we deliver them in a way that gives **insight**, makes the data **memorable**, and makes our audience **care**.

THE FACTS ARE THE FACTS.
BUT FOR A PRESENTATION, THAT'S NOT ENOUGH.

Imagine watching a football game with no ticking clock, no halftime, no surprises, and no announcers.

The facts are:

☐ These people . . .	00000 **000000**	
☐ move this ball . . .	0	
☐ this far . . .	← →	
☐ for this long . . .	60:00:00	
☐ and count how many times they do it.	X = ?	
☐ Yay.	zzzzz	

It wouldn't be very memorable.
(And we'd never watch football again.)

ORDER, EMPHASIS, AND COMMENTARY TURN THE FACTS INTO A LIVELY **STORY**.

WHY

And we're back to see who will take the bowl.

WHO + WHAT

Our starting lineup is a mix of rookies and veterans. Now THIS is football!

WHERE

The stadium here in Anaheim is packed.

WHEN

There's the kickoff. It's returned. It's a pass to . . .

HOW

You've got to admire the strategy we see here tonight.

HOW MUCH

UNBELIEVABLE FINISH!

See you again next Monday . . .

A REPORT PRESENTS THE DATA FOR THE FASTEST INSIGHT AND GREATEST RETENTION.

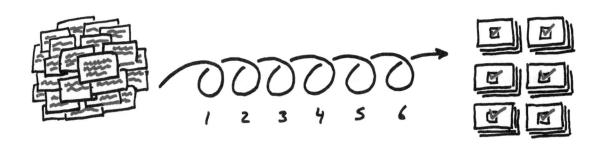

A nearly foolproof way to do that is to use **"6-Mode Thinking."**

MEET 6-MODE THINKING.

6-Mode Thinking is the cognition model that says that we can break almost any idea, problem, or story into six different yet complementary "modes" of information:

Who and what are we talking about?
Where are they located?
When do they occur?
How much is there?
How do they interact?
Why is this so?

6-MODE THINKING IS A TOOL.

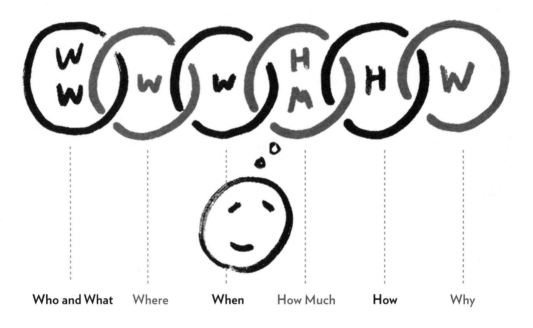

Who and What   Where   **When**   How Much   **How**   Why

Our mind works through all six modes all the time; they serve as the underlying structure we use to understand, recognize, and recall almost everything we learn.

6-MODE THINKING IS A LOOP.

A complete idea contains all six modes, linked together in a loop. The order of the six is not critical—after all, they all exist all the time—but "**Who and What**" or "**Why**" serve as the best starting points for a presentation.

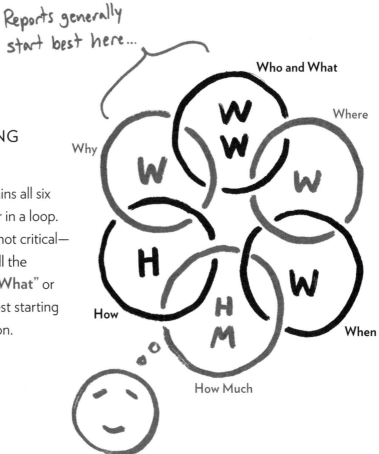

Reports generally start best here...

Who and What

Where

Why

When

How

How Much

EVERY GOOD REPORT IS A VARIATION OF THIS COMMON 6-MODE STORYLINE:

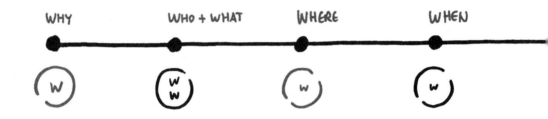

Why are we here?
To agree on this.

Who and What are we going to be talking about?
These are our players. These are the things in play.

Where are they located? Where are they going?
They are here and they overlap like this. This is where they will end up.

When do they interact?
The sequence of events is like this. This is when things happen.

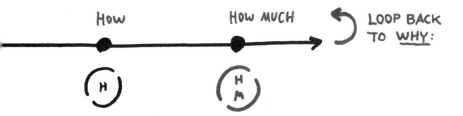

How does it occur?
This is how each impacts
the other.
This is the cause
and effect.

What are the numbers?
We have this many players.
We have this many things.
We have this much money.

The loop back: Did we meet
our original objective?
What do we need to do next?

These three sample **Reports** map to 6-Mode Thinking:

REPORT TITLE → **THE STATUS UPDATE**

(W)	The Why: (the objective)	We're here to get a better sense of where we are.
(WW)	Who and What:	Our company, our team, our product, our competitor.
(W W)	Where and When:	This segment, that segment; this quarter, that quarter.
(HM H)	How and How Much:	Rethink our strategy to drive our numbers up this much.

THE SPORTSCAST	HANS ROSLING'S 1ST TED TALK*
Follow the road to the Super Bowl.	Many smart people don't seem to understand poverty.
The teams, the players, the game.	Data on nations, mothers, children, wealth, and death.
This stadium, these plays, these downs.	The entire world; the entire 20th century.
Yardage, time-outs, punts, touchdowns!	Education = wealth; wealth = longer life.

*From TED 2006 and still the best Data Report ever filmed. (Also, unique among TED Talks, which tend to be dramas. More on this later . . .)

PRACTICE REPORT: "PROJECT SYLVESTER"

OUR SCENARIO:

Our idea: As social media transforms the digital landscape, many businesses are looking at ways to open up e-commerce across platforms and social networks. Our company is working on a secret internal project to do just that.

Us: We work for a midsized software company. We are the lead team on a new product. We need to deliver a status report to company decision makers.

Our audience: We need to update management and program sponsors on the status of our project. We're one of many initiatives under way, so we need to be as quick and clear as possible—yet still make our needs known.

Hint: Just the facts . . . with a little story added in.

GOOD MORNING.

Show:

Project Syvester

Secret Projects Group
Development Update

Tell: Thank you for coming to our status update on Project Sylvester.

WHY ARE WE HERE?

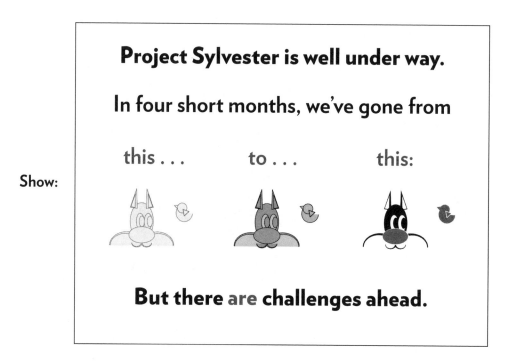

Show:

Project Sylvester is well under way.

In four short months, we've gone from

this . . .   to . . .   this:

But there are challenges ahead.

Tell: Project Sylvester is well under way. In just four months we've gone from an idea sketch to a well-functioning demo. That's good, but there are some challenges ahead.

WHY   WHO + WHAT   WHERE   WHEN   HOW   HOW MUCH   LOOP BACK TO WHY:

WHAT ARE WE TALKING ABOUT?

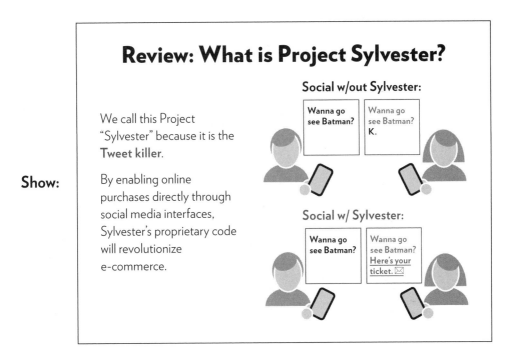

Review: What is Project Sylvester?

We call this Project "Sylvester" because it is the **Tweet killer**.

Show:

By enabling online purchases directly through social media interfaces, Sylvester's proprietary code will revolutionize e-commerce.

Social w/out Sylvester:

Wanna go see Batman?

Wanna go see Batman? K.

Social w/ Sylvester:

Wanna go see Batman?

Wanna go see Batman? Here's your ticket. ✉

Tell: Before we get into the details, here's a quick review. We call this Project Sylvester because this is the Tweet killer; that means Sylvester will enable people to make online purchases directly within their social media apps.

WHY · WHO + WHAT · WHERE · WHEN · HOW · HOW MUCH ↺ LOOP BACK TO WHY

WHO IS INVOLVED?

Show:

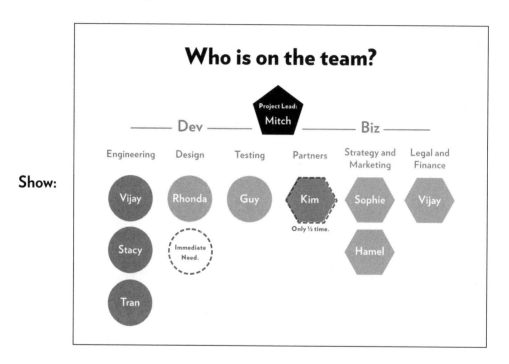

Who is on the team?

Project Lead: Mitch

—— Dev ——   —— Biz ——

| Engineering | Design | Testing | Partners | Strategy and Marketing | Legal and Finance |

Vijay, Rhonda, Guy, Kim, Sophie, Vijay

Stacy, Immediate Need., Hamel

Tran

Only ½ time.

Tell: I'm Mitch, and I'm the project lead. We've got a great team covering the development and business sides of Sylvester. But we're short one designer and our partnering lead is only half-time.

WHY · WHO + WHAT · WHERE · WHEN · HOW · HOW MUCH · LOOP BACK TO WHY.

WHERE ARE WE GOING?

Show:

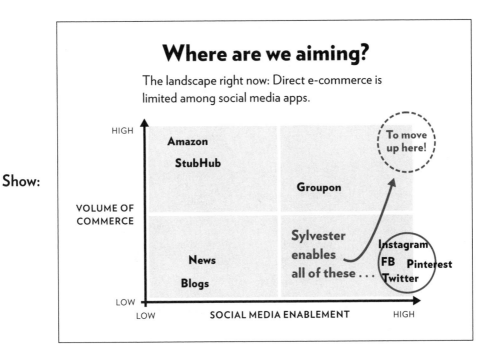

Where are we aiming?

The landscape right now: Direct e-commerce is
limited among social media apps.

- VOLUME OF COMMERCE (vertical axis: LOW to HIGH)
- SOCIAL MEDIA ENABLEMENT (horizontal axis: LOW to HIGH)

Amazon
StubHub

Groupon

To move up here!

News
Blogs

Sylvester enables all of these . . .

Instagram
FB   Pinterest
Twitter

Tell: If we look at the social media landscape, we see that none of the big
players have the capability to enable direct online sales. That's where
we come in—and that's why partnering is critical.

WHY   WHO + WHAT   WHERE   WHEN   HOW   HOW MUCH   LOOP BACK TO WHY!

WHERE ARE WE NOW?

Show:

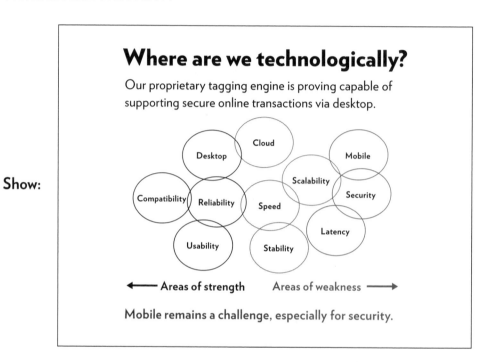

Where are we technologically?

Our proprietary tagging engine is proving capable of supporting secure online transactions via desktop.

Cloud

Desktop

Mobile

Scalability

Compatibility Reliability Speed Security

Latency

Usability Stability

← Areas of strength   Areas of weakness →

Mobile remains a challenge, especially for security.

Tell: Technologically, we've got a solid and scalable platform for the desktop. But mobile—especially security—is turning out to be our biggest challenge.

WHY   WHO + WHAT   **WHERE**   WHEN   HOW   HOW MUCH   LOOP BACK TO WHY:

WHEN DO THINGS HAPPEN?

Show:

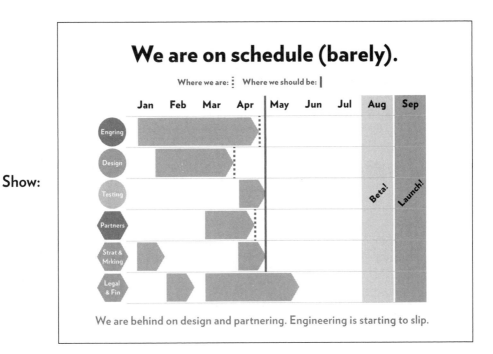

We are on schedule (barely).

Where we are: ⋮ Where we should be: |

	Jan	Feb	Mar	Apr	May	Jun	Jul	Aug	Sep
Engring									
Design									
Testing								Beta!	Launch!
Partners									
Strat & Mrking									
Legal & Fin									

We are behind on design and partnering. Engineering is starting to slip.

Tell: If we can resolve the mobile issue, we'll be pretty well on schedule for engineering. But being short a designer and partner lead is holding these two critical work streams back.

WHY · WHO + WHAT · WHERE · **WHEN** · HOW · HOW MUCH · LOOP BACK TO WHY

Show:

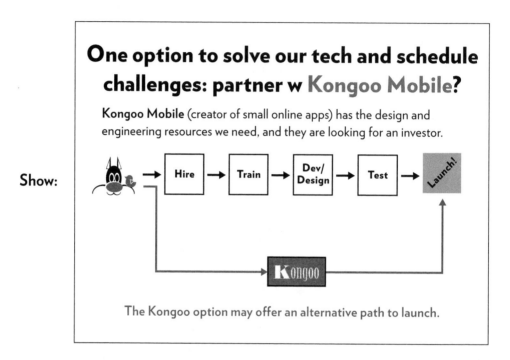

One option to solve our tech and schedule challenges: partner w Kongoo Mobile?

Kongoo Mobile (creator of small online apps) has the design and engineering resources we need, and they are looking for an investor.

Hire → Train → Dev/Design → Test → Launch!

Kongoo

The Kongoo option may offer an alternative path to launch.

Tell: There is one interesting new option. Word is that Kongoo Mobile— maker of a number of small but successful mobile apps—is looking for an investor. And they have the resources and tech we need. Partnering with them could accelerate us to launch.

WHY — WHO + WHAT — WHERE — WHEN — **How** — HOW MUCH — LOOP BACK TO WHY

HOW BIG IS THIS?

Show:

**The market opportunity is huge.
We want to be the first to launch.**

Tell: Getting to launch quickly is a key goal; we all know how big the potential market is for social e-commerce.

HOW MUCH ARE WE TALKING ABOUT?

Show:

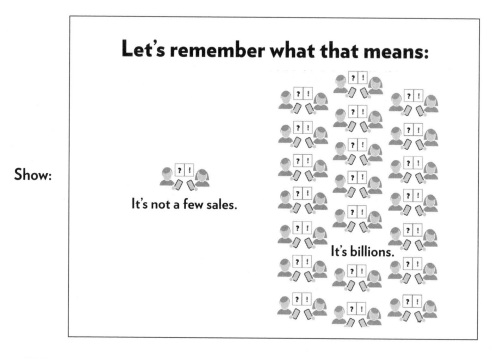

Let's remember what that means:

It's not a few sales.

It's billions.

Tell: That's because we're not talking about enabling a few social media transactions; we're talking about enabling billions.

WHY — WHO + WHAT — WHERE — WHEN — HOW — HOW MUCH — LOOP BACK TO WHY:

LOOP BACK TO WHY WE'RE HERE.

Show:

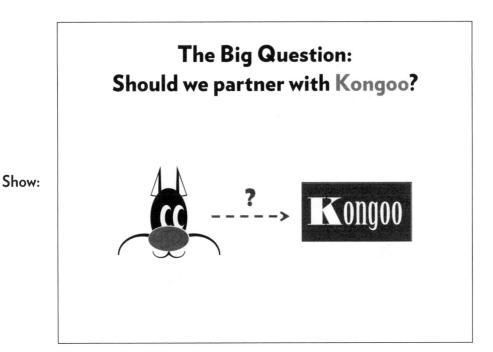

**The Big Question:
Should we partner with Kongoo?**

Tell: We can do it, but our big question is whether or not to partner with Kongoo.

Thanks for your time. Please let me know your thoughts on the new information mentioned.

WHY   WHO + WHAT   WHERE   WHEN   HOW   HOW MUCH   LOOP BACK TO WHY:

THE COMPLETE PRESENTATION MAPS TO THE **REPORT** STORYLINE.

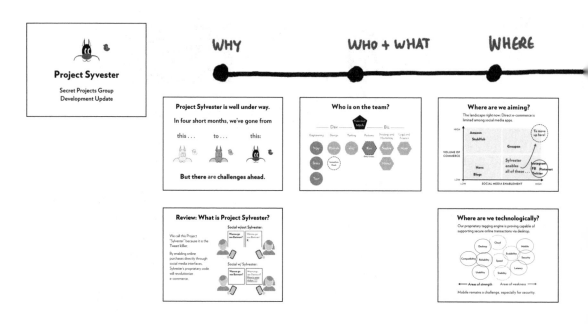

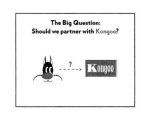

The Big Question:
Should we partner with Kongoo?

WHEN   HOW   HOW MUCH   LOOP BACK TO **WHY:**

We are on schedule (barely).

We are behind on design and partnering. Engineering is starting to slip.

One option to solve our tech and schedule challenges: partner w Kongoo Mobile?

Kongoo Mobile (creator of small online apps) has the design and engineering resources we need, and they are looking for an investor.

The Kongoo option may offer an alternative path to launch.

The market opportunity is huge. We want to be the first to launch.

Let's remember what that means:

It's not a few sales.

It's billions.

A REPORT CARD FOR OUR REPORT

1. Did we tell a true **story**?

2. Did we change our audience's **information**?

3. Are the facts **understandable**, insightful, and **memorable**?

HOW DID WE DO?

"Project Sylvester" is a fictionalized version of a report I worked on with a real tech start-up company a few years ago. (I've changed the names and technical details, as many companies continue to work on similar concepts.)

Outcome: This report helped secure the next round of financing, and the company went on to further develop their project. The future? Check your text messages . . .

A FEW FINAL THOUGHTS ON "THE REPORT"

The only time someone says, "Wow. What an extraordinary report," is when they have been changed.

An audience is changed when they see a connection they'd never seen before or understand something they never thought of before.

It's rare that someone gets promoted for just reciting the facts.

Data can be the most powerful truth, but data are rarely presented in a compelling enough way to make it past the boredom barrier. "Just the facts" make a good status report but rarely make an extraordinary presentation.

Turn the report into a sportscast. (But remember: We're the commentator, not the cheerleader.)

Announcers are passionate but not partisan. Although we may have a preferred point of view, we must present all the relevant data. If our audience perceives us as too biased, they will view our entire report with skepticism.

Whenever possible, push for one of the other storylines. They make for better presentations.

Just because our boss asks for a boring report, doesn't mean we have to give it to her. That's where our other storylines come in . . .

81

(Our PUMA ascends.)

The explanation shares knowledge: "Show me how."
With an explanation, we change our audience's knowledge or abilities.

EXPLANATIONS ARE EVERYWHERE.

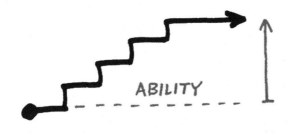

ABILITY

The EXPLANATION

Most presentations given at a conference, in a classroom, in a courtroom, or on an assembly line are intended to change the audience's **knowledge** or **abilities**: to explain what happened, provide new insight, or show a new way to do something.

- Training course
- Presenting a paper
- Introducing a process
- Self-help seminars
- Legal trials
- Sales training

Any explanation takes us to a new level of understanding. A great explanation makes it effortless.

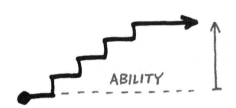

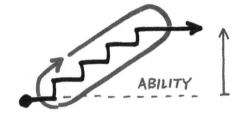

The EXPLANATION

The EXPLANATION

Any explanation is like a staircase, lifting the audience to a new level of understanding or ability.

A great explanation is like an escalator. The audience finds itself at the new level before it even knows it's moving.

Great explanations smoothly take us up to a new
level in three ways:

3. Each step is marked.
We provide a map of
the whole route in
advance, we preview
the steps, and
signpost as we go.

**When we reach the
top, we have a new
ability.**

**2. Each step leads
directly to the next.**
We start *here*, which
leads us to *there*, then
we add *that*, which we
top off with *this*.
Presto!

1. Each step is small.
New info comes in
bite-sized pieces, and
we don't move on until
we've had a chance to
chew.

We start at the base.

All good **explanations** follow this step-by-step storyline:

△ CHECKPOINTS

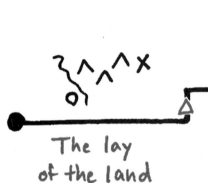

The lay of the land

Where are we now, where are we going, and what's between here and there?
Checkpoint:
Do we agree on our destination?

Our roadmap

Here is the route we'll take to get to our destination.
Checkpoint:
Do we agree on our route?

Our 1st step

Every journey begins with a step, and this is our first.
Checkpoint:
Are we all still together?

Our next steps...

Here's the next step . . . and the next, and so on . . .
Checkpoint: Do we know what we've done and where we are?

Almost there...

We're just about there. Let's take a look back over how far we've come.
Checkpoint: Do we see how much we've learned?

We've arrived!

We made it! We now have some new knowledge or ability.
Checkpoint: Can we repeat it on our own?

These three examples all follow the **explanation** storyline:

REPORT TITLE →

**HOW TO COOK
A MEAL**

	The lay of the land:	You've got a houseful to feed this Thanksgiving.
	The roadmap:	Appetizer, salad, main course, Jell-O, coffee.
	The steps . . .	**Preheat the oven to 250°F, prepare the stuffing, boil potatoes . . .**
	The destination:	The table is set and the guests are arriving. Clink!

THE TRUTH ABOUT WRITING A BOOK

INTRODUCING QUANTUM MECHANICS

THE TRUTH ABOUT WRITING A BOOK	INTRODUCING QUANTUM MECHANICS
You've had this idea rattling around for years.	The universe is a fascinating mystery.
Outline, write, edit, publish, promote.	Energy, mass, and light lead the way.
Put fingers on the keyboard and make them move. Again. And again . . .	Imagine a man on a train bouncing a ball . . .
NYT #1!	A deeper appreciation of the magic around us.

PRACTICE EXPLANATION: "THE FUTURE OF ACCOUNTING"

OUR SCENARIO (A TRUE STORY):

Our idea: Industry and government leaders realize there is a need to support education in science, technology, engineering, and math. As accountants, we believe this list must also include accounting.

Us: We're members of the American Accounting Association. The U.S. Department of the Treasury has asked us to work with other accounting organizations to design a roadmap for the future of accounting education.

Our audience: We're presenting our roadmap to other accounting professionals. Our goal is to help them understand the roadmap so that they may in turn present it to their peers, colleagues, and students.

GOOD MORNING.

Show:

Tell: It is our pleasure to introduce to you the "Pathways" findings: our roadmap for the future of accounting education.

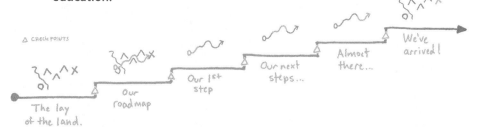

THE LAY OF THE LAND

Show:

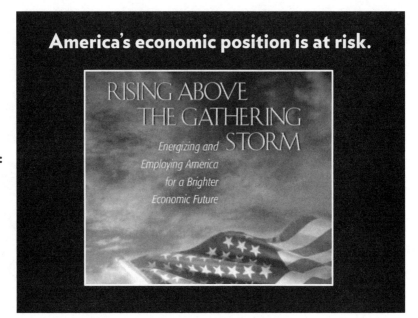

Tell: A decade ago, Congress looked at the future of American education and realized our economic position is at considerable risk to increasing foreign expertise and competition.

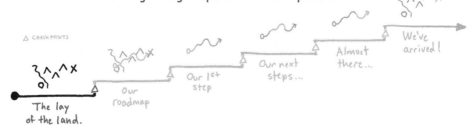

THE LAY OF THE LAND

Show:

> The good news is, we know what to do.
>
> Science   Technology   Engineering $\sqrt{x}$ Math

Tell: That report concluded by recommending increased support for education in the STEM disciplines: Science, Technology, Engineering, and Math.

△ CHECK POINTS

The lay of the land.

Our roadmap

Our 1st step

Our next steps...

Almost there...

We've arrived!

THE LAY OF THE LAND (CONTINUED)

Show:

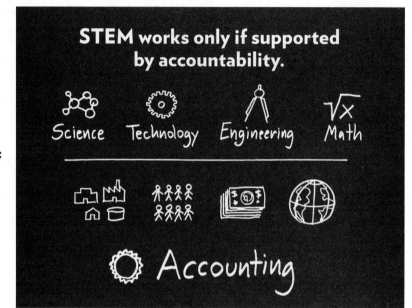

Tell: As accountants, we applaud that finding—and add another: Our STEM-based economy functions only if it is supported by trust and accountability.

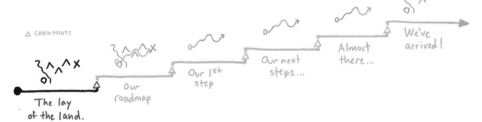

OUR ROADMAP

Show:

> **We believe that *Accounting* is the foundation of a free-market society.**
>
> STEM
> A
>
> – It's not so bad...
>
> (We can handle the pressure.)

Tell: We believe that accounting must again be recognized as the foundation of a flourishing free-market society.

△ CHECK POINTS

The lay of the land.

Our roadmap

Our 1st step

Our next steps...

Almost there...

We've arrived!

OUR ROADMAP (CONTINUED)

Show:

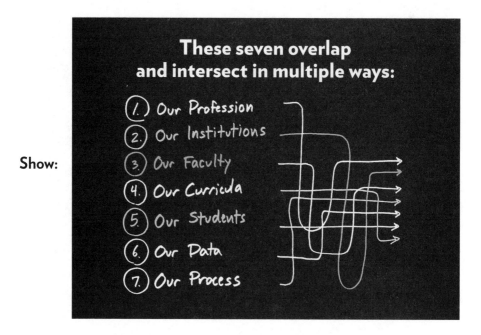

These seven overlap
and intersect in multiple ways:

1. Our Profession
2. Our Institutions
3. Our Faculty
4. Our Curricula
5. Our Students
6. Our Data
7. Our Process

Tell: To serve that role, the future of accounting education must account for seven overlapping paths.

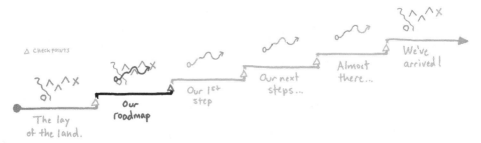

△ CHECK POINTS

The lay of the land.

Our roadmap

Our 1st step

Our next steps...

Almost there...

We've arrived!

OUR ROADMAP

Show:

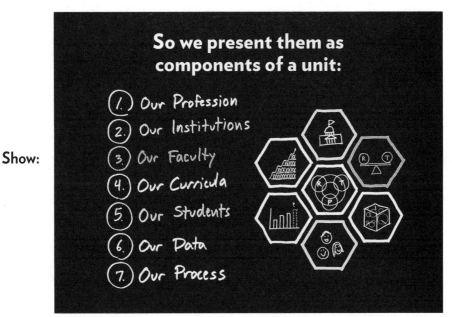

Tell: We believe these seven paths serve as individual components of the single entity we call "accounting." We'll now show you our recommendations for each component.

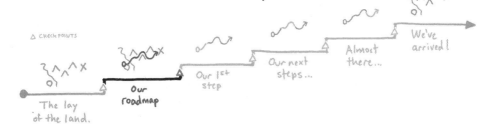

OUR FIRST STEP

Show:

Tell: We begin at the center, with the profession of accounting itself.

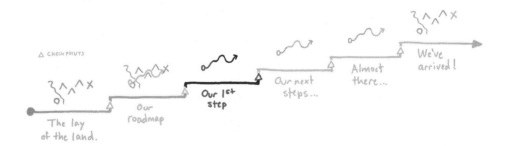

OUR FIRST STEP

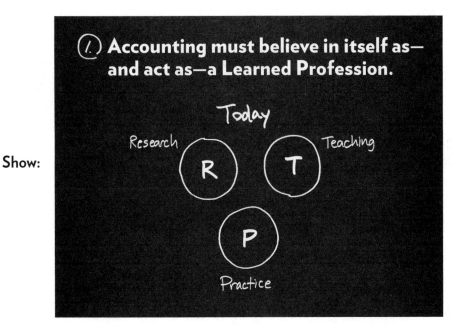

Show:

Tell: We believe that accounting must first establish itself as a truly learned profession.

OUR FIRST STEP (CONTINUED)

Show:

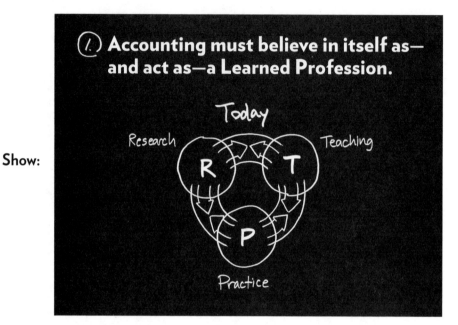

Tell: Which means we must look to strengthen the bonds that exist between the disciplines of research, teaching, and practice.

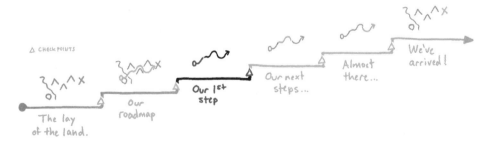

OUR NEXT STEPS . . .

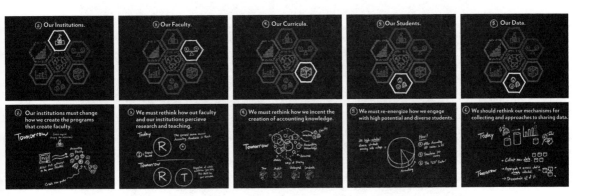

(We then go through the next five elements, each building upon the previous recommendation with one key insight and one key takeaway.)

ALMOST THERE . . .

Show:

Tell: The seventh and final recommendation goes to the heart of what we must do next: the process of implementing this plan.

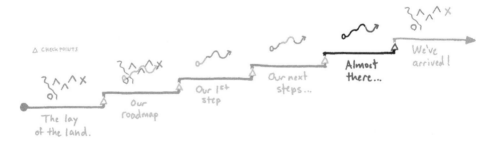

ALMOST THERE . . .

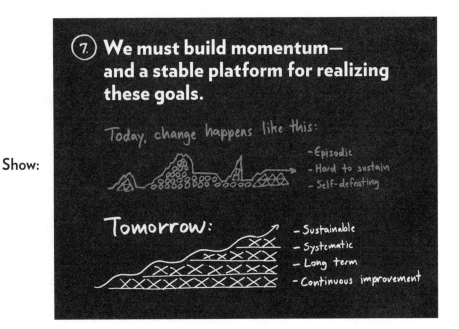

Show:

> ⑦ **We must build momentum—and a stable platform for realizing these goals.**
>
> Today, change happens like this:
> - Episodic
> - Hard to sustain
> - Self-defeating
>
> Tomorrow:
> - Sustainable
> - Systematic
> - Long term
> - Continuous improvement

Tell: To support momentum for these changes, we are building a stable platform upon which we can all find support and grow.

△ CHECKPOINTS

The lay of the land.

Our roadmap

Our 1st step

Our next steps...

Almost there...

We've arrived!

WE'VE ARRIVED!

Show:

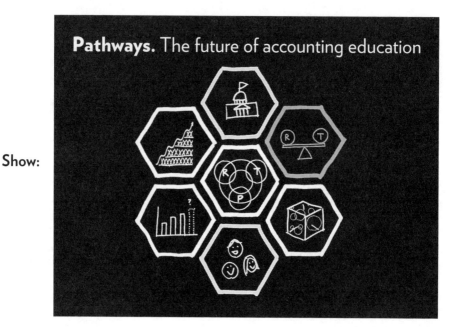

Pathways. The future of accounting education

Tell: Together, these seven components represent the heart of our future profession. We hope they are clear and make sense to you.

WE'VE ARRIVED!

Show:

Please join us to learn more about **Pathways.**

Tell: We invite you to join us as we roll out these recommendations across the industry over the coming months and years. Thank you.

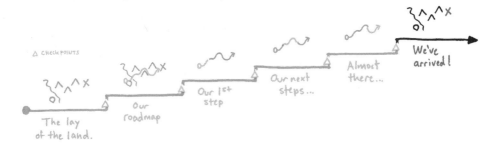

The complete presentation maps to the **explanation** storyline:

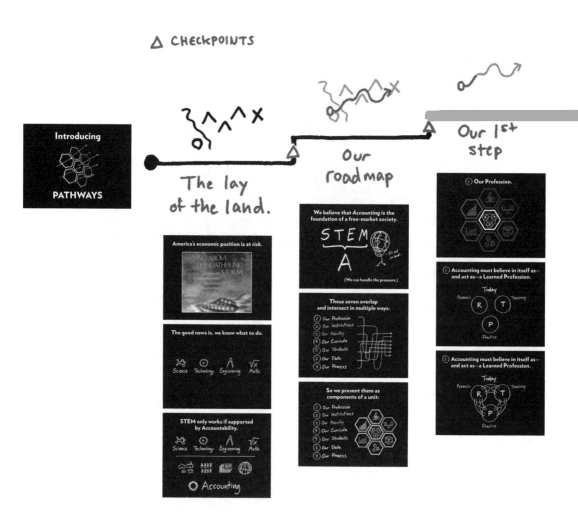

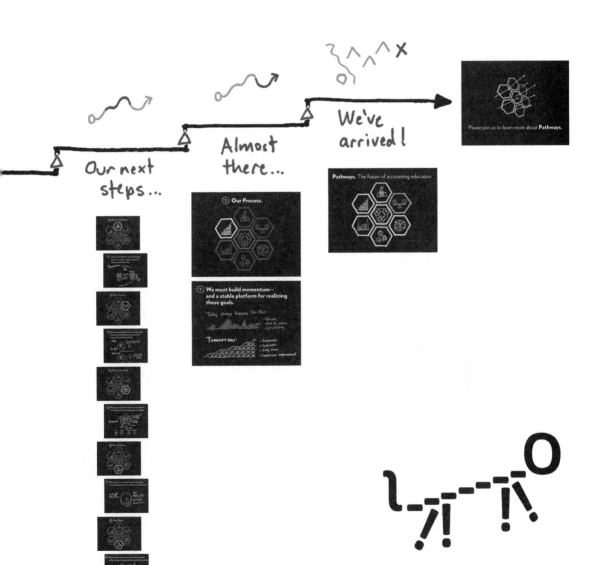

Our next steps...

Almost there...

We've arrived!

Our Process.

We must build momentum—
and a stable platform for realizing
these goals.

Pathways. The future of accounting education

Please join us to learn more about **Pathways.**

A REPORT CARD FOR OUR EXPLANATION

1. Did we tell a true **story**?

2. Did we change our audience's **knowledge** or **ability**?

3. Is the new ability straightforward enough to **practice** and practical enough to **apply**?

HOW DID WE DO?

This is the actual presentation we developed to communicate the "Pathways" recommendations to the thousands of accounting professionals who will support it over the coming years. This 30-minute presentation summarized 136 pages of written material into a single, memorable deck. It has since been delivered hundreds of times by dozens of speakers at events across the country.

Outcome: The response has been, well, extraordinary.

A FEW FINAL THOUGHTS ON "THE EXPLANATION"

There is no such thing as a boring topic. There is only boring teaching. Any subject can be made fascinating by simply making it clear. Clarity comes from breaking the complex into individual steps, then recombining those steps one by one.

"Getting it" is the ultimate rush. When we suddenly "see" something we've been struggling to understand, we get a blast of dopamine equal to a huge slice of chocolate cake. It's our own brain rewarding us for making sense of complexity.

Whether describing a new discovery or showing the audience how to bake a cake, the essential explanation process remains the same. If we take our audience with us one step at a time—and have frequent checkpoints to ensure we're all together—it is possible to explain almost anything in a way almost anyone understands.

If given the option, deliver an explanation rather than a report. A clear explanation makes data become useful, applicable knowledge. This moves information to understanding, which is a far more memorable and actionable place.

(Our PUMA pounces.)

The pitch poses a problem and a solution, but it requires some persuasion: "Convince me."

With a pitch, we change our audience's actions.

THE **PITCH** GETS US OVER A HURDLE.

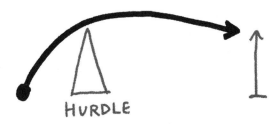

The **PITCH**

Most presentations given on the sales floor, in the boardroom, at the client meeting, at the venture capital firm, or at the political rally are intended to change the audience's **actions**: Give money or support, buy something new, or do something different.

- Sales pitch
- Dog and pony show
- Gentle persuasion
- Ask for money
- Request assistance
- Launch a product

IF WE DO THE PITCH RIGHT . . .

We make a pitch by establishing **common ground** with our audience, stating a **common problem** that we all recognize, and then providing a **new solution** that fixes, eliminates, or leaps past the problem.

If our pitch is convincing, our audience *buys* **our idea and takes the action we recommend.**

PITCHES: HARDBALL VS. SOFTBALL

OLD SCHOOL WAS HARDBALL

In the old days, pitching was viewed as a me-against-you proposition. Buyers and sellers played on opposite sides of the plate, and only one could win.

Hardball works fine when problems are plenty and solutions are limited—but when the game is over, one team always feels lousy.

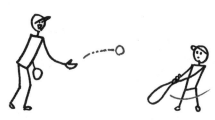

NEW SCHOOL IS SOFTBALL

Pitching today is a different world. Buyers and sellers both have so many options that it proves far more effective to work together.

Softball pitching means we're on the same team, working together to get the highest mutual score. When we're done, everyone feels better.

ALL SOFTBALL PITCHES CONTAIN A VARIATION
OF THE SAME ESSENTIAL PARTS:

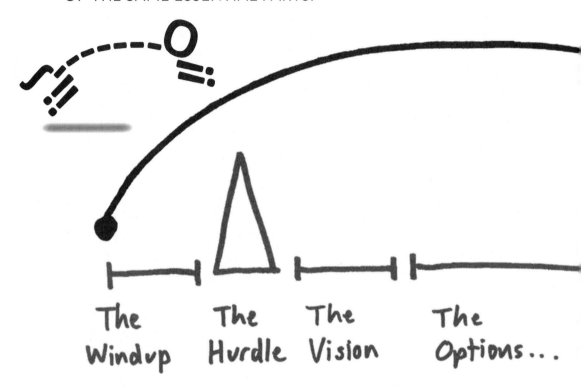

The
Windup

The
Hurdle

The
Vision

The
Options...

The windup:
We start with a
quick summary of
where we are today.

The hurdle:
We introduce
a problem we're
all facing.

The vision:
We show a glimpse
of a way over the
problem.

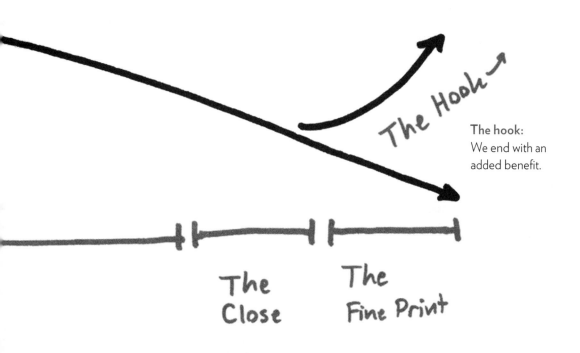

The hook:
We end with an
added benefit.

The options:
We present two ways to
reach the vision—a boring
one and an inspiring one.

The close:
We show why the
inspiring option is
really the only option.

The fine print:
With our audience excited,
we cover the details of how
we make it happen.

These Three Examples All Follow the **Pitch** Storyline:

CALOOPA COFFEE

The Windup: **(Our common ground)**	We'd all love to feel energized and awake right now.
The Hurdle: (The shared problem)	We're beat.
Solution: **(The inspiring option)**	Caloopa Coffee is steaming hot and tastes like heaven.
The Close	Buy a cup of Caloopa. (And WiFi is free!)

STAY UP LATE

PHONES SUCK

We all want me to be a happy, well-adjusted kid, right?	We want to keep in touch and we want it to be fun.
It's Saturday night.	Mobile phones suck.
I go to the movies with my friends while you and Dad stay here and relax.	A phone + a music player + mobile Internet.
Give me $60 and permission to call Amy. (Yes, I have my phone!)	**Get an iPhone. Now. (Okay, that's a little bit hardball, but he *was* Steve Jobs.)**

PRACTICE PITCH: "THE BITTER PILL"

OUR SCENARIO:

Our idea: As health care reform becomes reality, we must initiate changes to the underlying infrastructure of our business systems. These changes are expensive—but if we don't make them, our company won't be able to support future growth.

Us: We are a senior technical engineer at a large health care company. We design and build the computer systems that keep our company going.

Our audience: We need to convince senior management to provide additional funding to our group—which is tricky, because they're already pressed to spend more money on improving daily patient care. In other words, we've got to sell an expensive but necessary long-term change to a group of stressed executives.

Hint: A spoonful of sugar helps the medicine go down . . .

GOOD AFTERNOON.

Show:

> **_All for one and one for all._**
>
>
>
> # The Case for an Integrated Data Strategy

Tell: Good afternoon, colleagues. Thank you for letting me share my team's thoughts on the need for an integrated data strategy.

THE WINDUP . . .

Show:

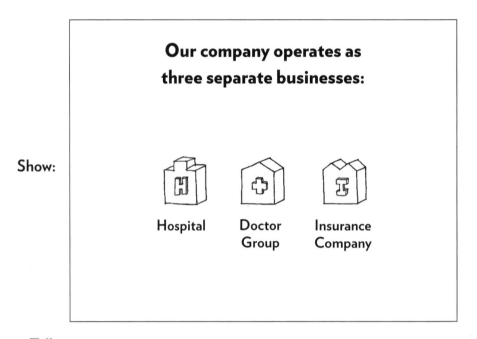

Our company operates as three separate businesses:

Hospital   Doctor Group   Insurance Company

Tell: Today we act as three separate businesses: our hospitals, our doctor groups, and our insurance company.

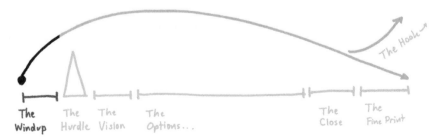

THE WINDUP . . .

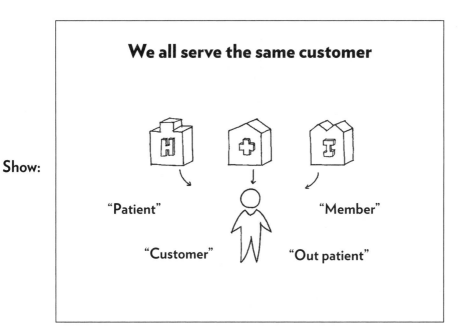

We all serve the same customer

Show:

"Patient"

"Member"

"Customer"

"Out patient"

Tell: We all serve the same customer, but depending on our business, we might see a "guest" or a "patient" or a "member."

The Windup   The Hurdle   The Vision   The Options...   The Close   The Fine Print   The Hook

THE WINDUP (CONTINUED) . . .

Show:

But we all see that customer a little differently:

Tell: From the data we collect, we all see that same customer a little differently.

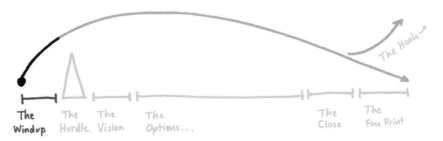

The Hook

The Windup | The Hurdle | The Vision | The Options... | The Close | The Fine Print

THE HURDLE

Show:

Tell: That will no longer work. Powerful forces—from health care reform to new payment systems—are forcing us to look at our customer in a new way.

THE VISION

Show:

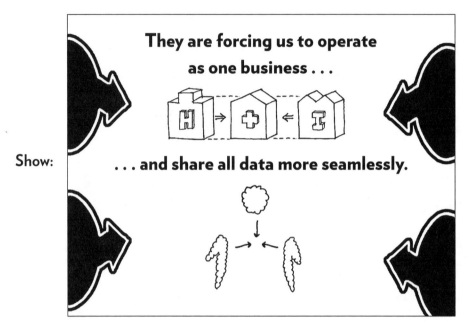

They are forcing us to operate as one business . . .

. . . and share all data more seamlessly.

Tell: Those forces mean two things: **1.** We must operate more like one business. **2.** We must share customer data seamlessly.

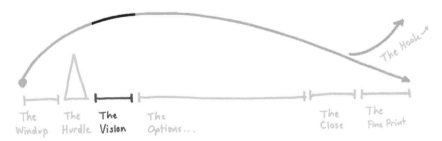

The Windup — The Hurdle — **The Vision** — The Options... — The Close — The Fine Print — The Hook

THE OPTIONS . . .

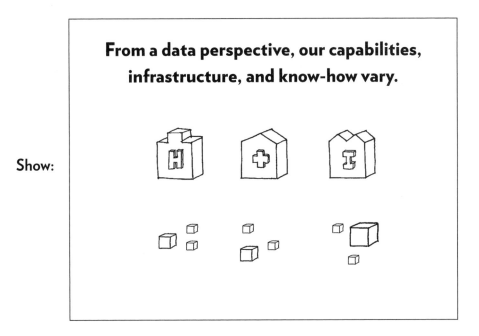

From a data perspective, our capabilities, infrastructure, and know-how vary.

Show:

Tell: From a data perspective, each of our businesses has certain areas of expertise, capacity, and insight—and they're not the same.

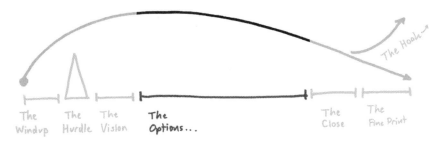

The Windup | The Hurdle | The Vision | **The Options...** | The Close | The Fine Print

The Hook

ONE POSSIBLE OPTION

Show:

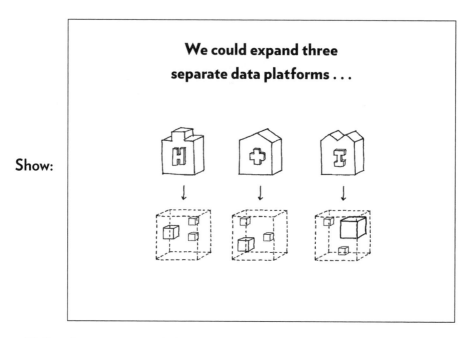

We could expand three separate data platforms . . .

Tell: One option is to help each of our businesses grow their own customer data system.

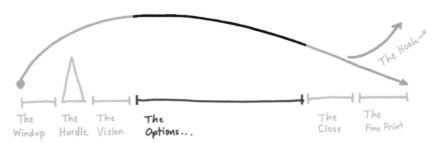

The Windup   The Hurdle   The Vision   **The Options...**   The Close   The Fine Print   The Hook →

A BETTER OPTION

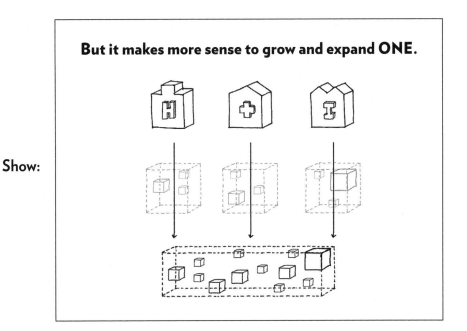

But it makes more sense to grow and expand ONE.

Show:

Tell: A better option is to help our businesses build one complete data
system, where each can access all the information they need.

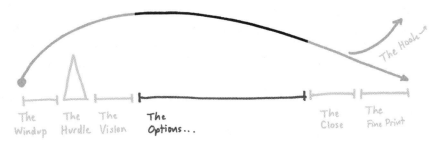

The   The   The   The   The   The
Windup   Hurdle   Vision   Options...   Close   Fine Print

THE CLOSE

Show:

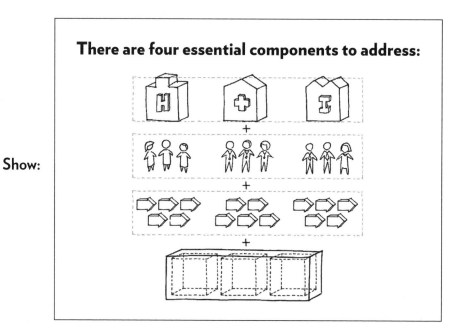

> **There are four essential components to address:**

Tell: To do this, we'd need to account for four things: **1.** Individual business needs **2.** Individual employee needs **3.** Individual business processes **4.** A common platform

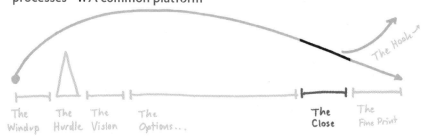

THE CLOSE

Show:

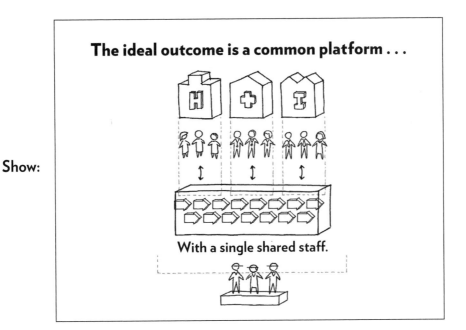

The ideal outcome is a common platform . . .

With a single shared staff.

Tell: Putting those together would give us something unique: a single centralized data system accessible by all, yet managed by a small shared group.

The Windup | The Hurdle | The Vision | The Options... | The Close | The Fine Print | The Hook

THE FINE PRINT

Show:

Tell: To do this will require two years of hard work and a lot of money, but it will pay off in future growth and future savings.

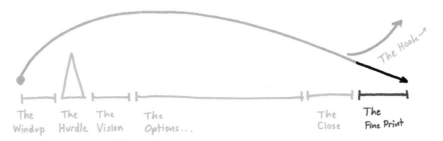

THE HOOK

Show:

If we do this right, we'll set the national standard!

Tell: If we do this now, we will be one of the first groups in the country ready to face the future of health care. Thank you.

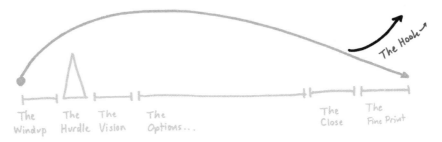

The Windup | The Hurdle | The Vision | The Options... | The Close | The Fine Print | The Hook

The Complete Presentation Maps
to the **Pitch** Storyline:

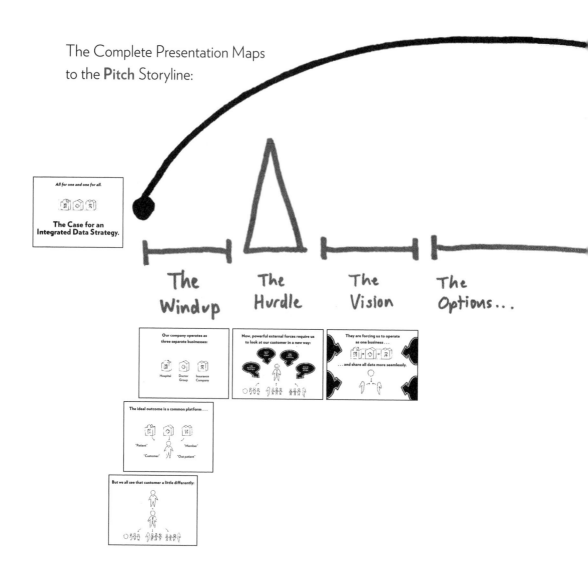

The
Windup

The
Hurdle

The
Vision

The
Options...

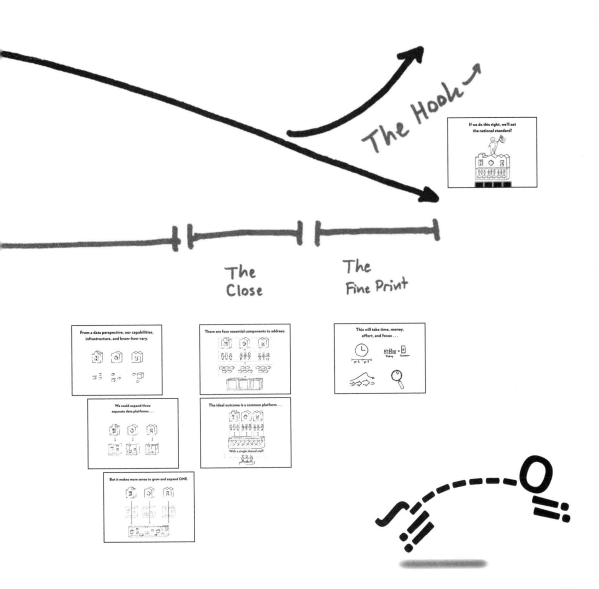

The Hook →

If we do this right, we'll set the national standard!

The Close

The Fine Print

From a data perspective, our capabilities, infrastructure, and know-how vary.

There are four essential components to address:

This will take time, money, effort, and focus . . .

We could expand three separate data platforms . . .

The ideal outcome is a common platform . . .

With a single shared staff.

But it makes more sense to grow and expand ONE.

A REPORT CARD FOR OUR PITCH

1. Did we tell a true **story**?

2. Did we change our audience's **actions**?

3. Is the new action one that benefits both **us** and our **audience**?

HOW DID WE DO?

This is an abbreviated version of a presentation I developed with a health care organization facing this actual challenge. We created this version because the first presentation—a typically flat report—failed to convey the urgency of the problem and the clarity of the proposed solution.

Outcome: Our revised "pitch" version secured the initial multimillion-dollar investment for the common data platform test program.

A FEW FINAL THOUGHTS ON "THE PITCH"

The key to the softball pitch is to establish common ground with our audience.

The essence of any pitch is to get our audience to try something new. But in most cases, something truly "new" is the last thing people really want. We first need to establish that *there is a problem*—and that it is a *problem we share*.

This is why it is almost impossible for someone unfamiliar with a problem to sell a solution; our audience can tell we're not telling the *truth*.

If we want to sell a solution, we first have to truly know the problem.

All presentations "sell," but only the pitch places the sale front and center.

All our presentations make a "sale" of some kind: The report "sells" new information, the explanation "sells" new abilities, and the drama, as we'll soon see, "sells" emotion.

But it's the pitch in which the "sale" is the point. And that's okay. Why?

Because our audience knows when they're being sold something. If we're up front about it, they won't mind. They'll even pounce with us.

(Our PUMA leaps.)

The drama takes us on a journey: "First make me cry, then make me laugh."
With a drama, we change our audience's beliefs.

THE **DRAMA** BREAKS OUR HEART, THEN MENDS IT.

Most presentations given as conference keynotes, sermons in church, TED Talks, or told around the campfire are intended to change the audience's beliefs: to help the participants look at the world differently, to become better people, to have greater compassion or understanding.

- The perfect conference keynote
- 90% of all TED Talks
- The spiritual revival
- The tale of our own personal journey
- Bad news delivered really well
- Great news delivered unforgettably

THE DRAMA IS AN ADVENTURE, MYTH, AND LIFE LESSON ALL ROLLED INTO ONE.

The drama is the grandmother of all presentations. Greek myths, Hindu Upanishads, African legends, and the Bible: All started as stories one person *presented* to another.

Although the individual stories are different, they all have two things in common: They tell a **truth**, and they tell it according to a single, classic **structure**.

Historian Joseph Campbell identified a simple structure common to myths from around the world. He called this the "Hero's Journey" and illustrated it with a single circle.

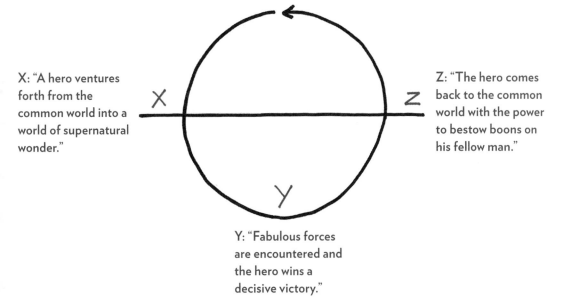

X: "A hero ventures forth from the common world into a world of supernatural wonder."

Z: "The hero comes back to the common world with the power to bestow boons on his fellow man."

Y: "Fabulous forces are encountered and the hero wins a decisive victory."

If our drama tells a truth and follows a variation of this classic structure, our audience can't help but be moved.

THE CLASSIC STRUCTURE OF GREAT DRAMA FOLLOWS THIS SIMPLE LINE:

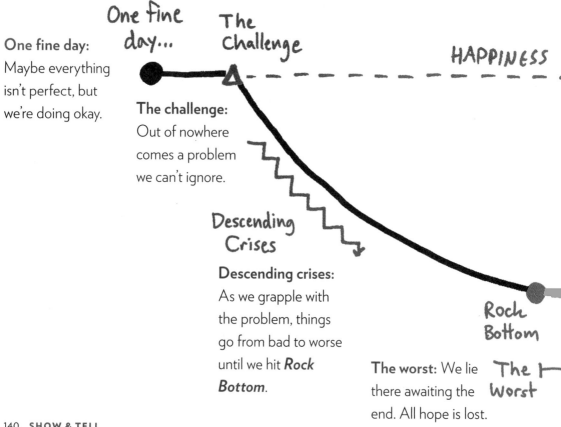

One fine day: Maybe everything isn't perfect, but we're doing okay.

The challenge: Out of nowhere comes a problem we can't ignore.

Descending crises: As we grapple with the problem, things go from bad to worse until we hit **Rock Bottom**.

The worst: We lie there awaiting the end. All hope is lost.

One fine day...

The Challenge

HAPPINESS

Descending Crises

Rock Bottom

The Worst

The Lesson

The lesson: We come away with a new gift that we'll never forget.

The Return!

The return: We don't just make it home, we burst through into a whole new world of possibility.

The Rise

The rise: Through abilities we never knew we had, we fight our way back to the surface.

The Discovery

The discovery: Wait a minute, what's this? We suddenly see a way out.

Here are three sample **dramas** that follow the storyline:

LITTLE RED HOOD

One fine day . . .	Little Red is taking a basket to Grandma's house.
The challenge:	**The forest is dark and scary.**
Descending crises:	Where's Grandma? What big teeth you have. Gulp.
Discovery and return:	**The hunter kills the wolf and Little Red is reunited with Grandma.**

THE HERO BOSS	**JILL BOLTE TAYLOR'S INSIGHT***
The company is going like gangbusters.	The neuroscientist is at the top of her game.
The market tanks.	**She suffers a debilitating stroke.**
The company is going under. Heads roll. Products fail.	She loses memory, speech, and knows she is dying.
The boss finds a new niche, reinvests her own money, and gets on the cover of the *WSJ*.	**Eight years later, her reborn mind shows her how to really live.**

*From TED 2008; one of the most watched TED Talks ever, the one that set the bar for TED "dramas" ever since.

PRACTICE DRAMA:
"OUT OF AIR" (A TRUE STORY)

OUR SCENARIO:

The idea: Ten years ago in Moscow, I interviewed the first man to walk in space. His name was Alexei Leonov, and he told me the most incredible story of his adventure of forty years before.

Me (this is my own true life story): I graduated from the university with majors in biology and painting. I began a career in graphic design that took me around the world, including Russia.

The audience: Last year, I was asked to share an inspiring science or art story at an alumni fund-raiser for my alma mater. I decided to tell Alexei's tale, because it covered both. I had never shared this story in public before.

This is that presentation.

Hint: Take a deep breath and close your eyes . . .

GOOD EVENING.

Show:

A few years ago, I met the most interesting man.

Tell: A few years ago while traveling in Russia, I met a most interesting man. Over the course of an afternoon, he told me an incredible story from forty years before.

ONE FINE DAY . . .

A painter . . .

Show:

Tell: Trained as a scientist and pilot, he also loved to paint.

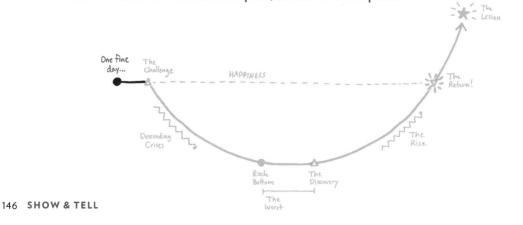

One fine day...
The Challenge
HAPPINESS
The Lesson
The Return!
Descending Crises
The Rise
Rock Bottom
The Discovery
The Worst

ONE FINE DAY . . .

Show:

Cosmonaut Alexei Leonov

Tell: But painting was for him just a hobby. Because he was Major Alexei Leonov, Soviet cosmonaut.

One fine day... The Challenge — HAPPINESS — The Return!

The Lesson

Descending Crises

Rock Bottom — The Discovery

The Rise

The Worst

THE CHALLENGE

Show:

March 18, 1965.

Tell: During the height of the space race, Alexei was selected to lead the most audacious and risky space flight ever attempted.

One fine day...

The Challenge

HAPPINESS

The Lesson

The Return!

Descending Crises

The Rise

Rock Bottom

The Discovery

The Worst

THE CHALLENGE

Show:

Tell: On the morning of March 18, 1965, Alexei lifted off from
the secret Baikonur Cosmodrome, deep in the Soviet Union.

DESCENDING CRISES . . .

Show:

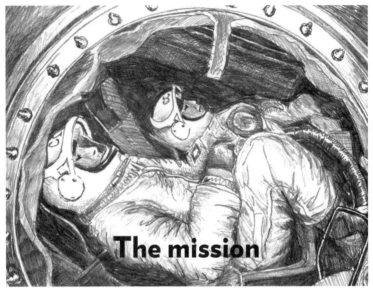

The mission

Tell: With Major Pavel Belyayev commanding the ship, Alexei's role was to exit into open space. It was to be the first space walk in history.

One fine day...
The Challenge
HAPPINESS
The Lesson
The Return!
Descending Crises
The Rise
Rock Bottom
The Discovery
The Worst

DESCENDING CRISES . . .

Show:

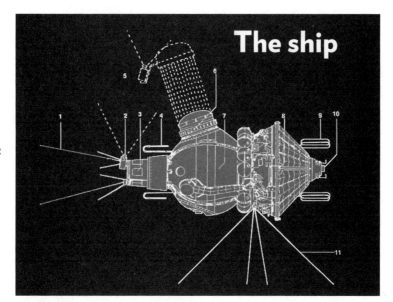

Tell: The ship, although a reliable design, was already obsolete and had been jerry-rigged to meet the incredible demands of the flight.

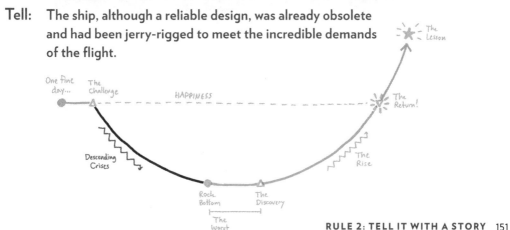

THE MOMENT OF TRUTH

Show:

The moment of truth

Tell: Three hours into the flight, Alexei gave his suit a final pressure check, then stepped into open space.

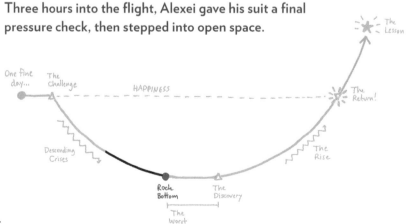

THINGS WENT FROM MAGNIFICENT . . .

Show:

Tell: Alexei was overwhelmed with the view. There below him lay the entire planet Earth, seemingly close enough to touch.

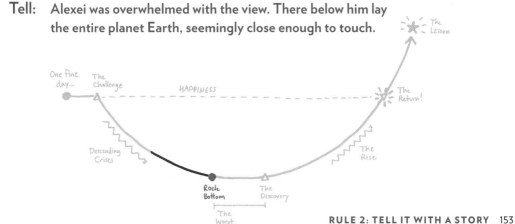

. . . TO DISASTER

Show:

Tell: But success was short-lived. Within seconds, Alexei realized his suit was overinflating. "Just like the Michelin man," he told me.

One fine day... The Challenge

HAPPINESS

The Lesson

The Return!

Descending Crises

The Rise

Rock Bottom

The Discovery

The Worst

. . . TO DISASTER

Show:

I can't get back in.

Tell: As his suit expanded, Alexei gave up on his science tasks and focused on survival. But he knew that with no control over his suit, he couldn't get back into the ship.

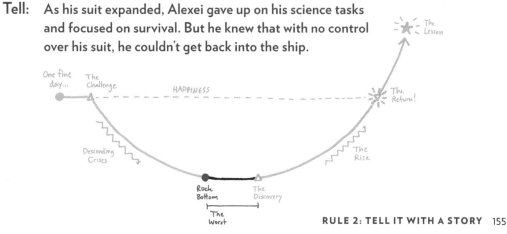

IT WAS THE END.

Show:

I close
my eyes.

Tell: Then he told me, "I know it is over. So I close my eyes."

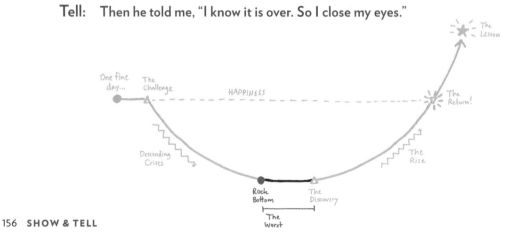

ROCK BOTTOM

Show:

I am going to die.

Tell: "I am going to die."

THE DISCOVERY

Show:

Then I see it!

Tell: But then, in his mind's eye, a possibility emerged; something never before tested, never even discussed.

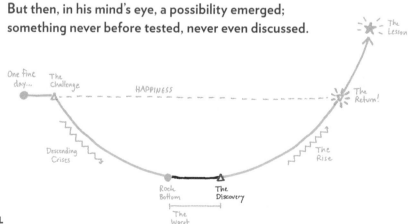

THE DISCOVERY

Show:

Tell: Then sitting in the room with me in Moscow, Alexei picked up his pen and as he talked, he began to draw . . .

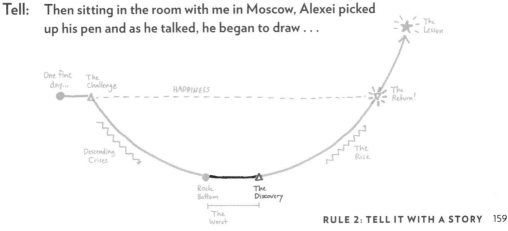

THE DISCOVERY (CONTINUED)

Show:

"I'm too ballooned to get in."

Tell: "I knew that I was too ballooned to fit back into the air lock door, which I couldn't even see. I knew I needed to deflate my suit, but that would be instant death."

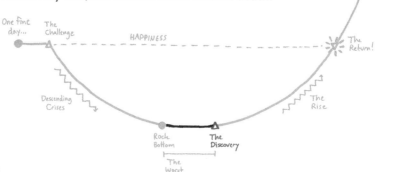

THE RISE

Show:

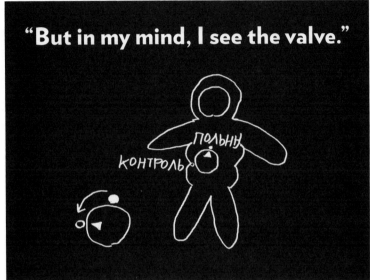

"But in my mind, I see the valve."

ПОЛЬНИ
КОНТРОЛЬ

Tell: "Or would it? In my mind's eye, I saw the test pressurization valve on my suit. It was only there for use on the ground, but I thought 'Why not?'"

One fine day...   The Challenge   *HAPPINESS*   The Return!

The Lesson

Descending Crises

The Rise

Rock Bottom   The Discovery

The Worst

THE RISE (CONTINUED)

"I let out all my air."

Show:

Tell: "I didn't say anything to Mission Control; they'd just tell me 'No.' So I forced my hand down to the valve and turned it. I let my air out into space."

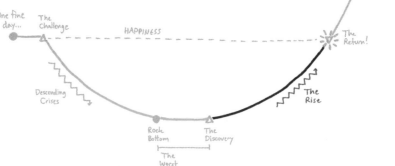

THE RETURN

Show:

"I fit!"

Tell: "It worked! My suit deflated. I had seconds to get back in. Somehow I entered the hatch, turned around, and got my feet into the ship."

One fine day... | The Challenge

HAPPINESS — The Return!

The Lesson

Descending Crises

Rock Bottom

The Discovery

The Worst

The Rise

THE RETURN (CONTINUED)

Show:

I made it home.

TIME

CCCP

OUTSIDE IN SPACE

March 25, 1965

Tell: "Pavel yanked me in by the feet and closed the hatch. We made it home." *Time* magazine put Alexei's adventure on the cover, and no one ever knew how close it was.

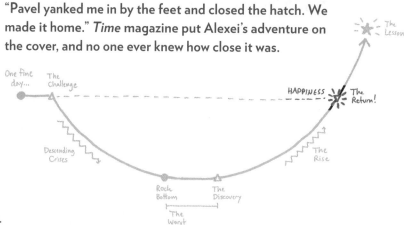

THE LESSON

Show:

"**Don't ever give up.**

**As long as you keep looking,
you will always find a way.**"

Tell: Then Alexei told me what he learned up there. "Daniel, don't ever give up. As long as you keep looking, you will always find a way."

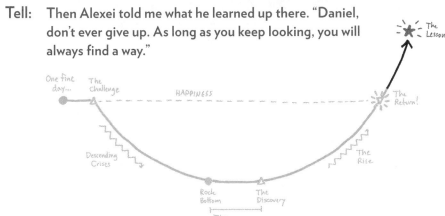

THE COMPLETE PRESENTATION MAPS TO THE "DRAMA" STORYLINE:

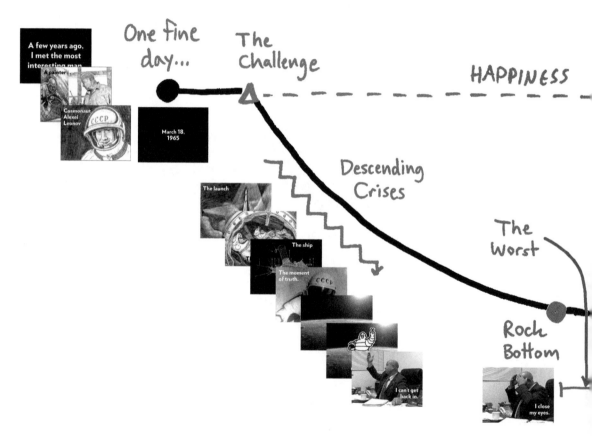

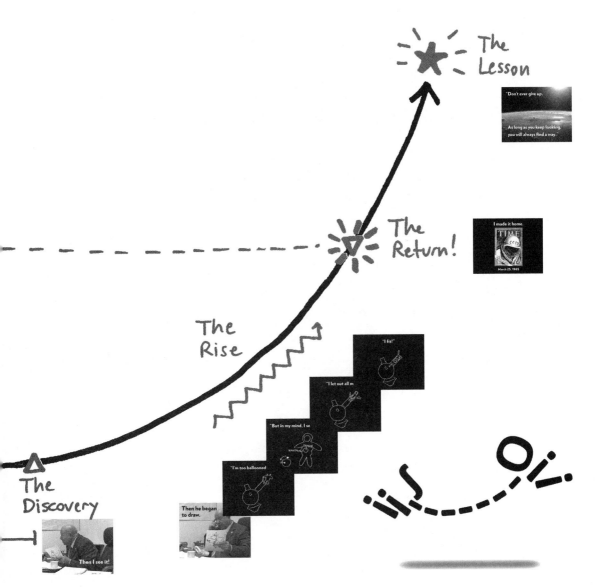

The Lesson

"Don't ever give up.

As long as you keep looking,
you will always find a way."

The
Return!

I made it home.

TIME

March 25, 1965

The
Rise

"I fit!"

"I let out all m

"But in my mind, I se

"I'm too ballooned

Then he began
to draw.

The
Discovery

Then I see it!

A REPORT CARD FOR OUR DRAMA

1. Did we tell a true **story**?

2. Did we change or reinforce our audience's **beliefs**?

3. Are these beliefs likely to be **recalled** and **savored**?

HOW DID WE DO?

The goal of the presentation was to share a story about art and science that might inspire the audience to donate to the university. I loved sharing Alexei's story, and the audience loved it too. How do I know they did?

Outcome: The university collected almost a quarter million dollars that night.

A FEW FINAL THOUGHTS ON "THE DRAMA"

Adding a bit of drama to the other storylines is always a good idea. We often like to think of ourselves—especially in business—as cold, calculating fact machines. While that may sometimes feel true, it never really is.

So when appropriate, feel free to throw in a bit of drama to that report, explanation, or pitch. It could be just the thing to help someone take their own flying leap.

There is no more powerful presentation we can deliver than the drama.

Because the drama reaches into our heart, it resonates at the highest level of the truth pyramid. Which means if we hit it just right, the change we trigger can last forever.

One final thought on storylines . . . Whichever storyline we choose, it serves as the guide rope from our mind to our audience's experience.

As presenters, it is our job to keep this line taut and moving.

Our storylines are strong, but they can be broken. And that's when we lose our audience.

As presenters, we want to *avoid*:

~~Knotting the line~~
(Our storyline becomes too complex.)

~~Allowing too much slack~~
(Our storyline becomes flabby.)

~~Breaking the line~~
(Our storyline loses continuity.)

TO KEEP OUR STORYLINE TIGHT, WE STACK IT IN A SINGLE DECK.

The deck is our complete presentation in a single stand-alone document. The deck contains our entire story and all details on a series of slides that flow smoothly in order from beginning to end.

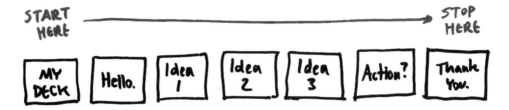

TO KEEP OUR SLIDES TIGHT, WE LIMIT EACH TO A SINGLE IDEA— AND THAT IS ALL.

The ideal slide contains:

- A headline
- A picture
- A brief caption
- Nothing else

ANY SLIDE THAT BREAKS THE CONTINUITY OF OUR STORYLINE IS A **BAD SLIDE**.

During our presentation, single slides that try to explain multiple ideas are the fastest way to break our storyline and lose or confuse the audience.

 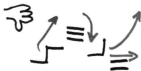

IF AN IDEA IS TOO COMPLICATED TO EXPLAIN WITH ONE SLIDE, THEN WE BREAK IT INTO SEVERAL SLIDES:

Any level of complexity can be clarified by presenting the idea as a "build."

THE OTHER WAY TO KEEP THE LINE TAUT
IS TO SHOW PICTURES.

Keep it crisp. Stay frosty. How? Say less, show more.

CHAPTER 4

RULE 3: TELL THE STORY WITH PICTURES

Lead with the eye and the mind will follow.

> I rarely think in words at all. My visual images have to be translated laboriously into conventional verbal and mathematical terms.
>
> **—ALBERT EINSTEIN**

> I have drawn a map . . . It's one of the first things I did.
>
> **—J. K. ROWLING**

MORE OF OUR BRAIN IS DEDICATED TO VISION THAN TO ANY OTHER THING THAT WE DO.

More of the brain is devoted to vision and visual processing than any other known function, including language. More neurons in the human brain are involved in vision than is the case of all the other sensory modalities combined.

DR. LEO CHALUPA

Dr. Leo M. Chalupa is vice president for research and professor of Pharmacology and Physiology at George Washington University. He was previously a Distinguished Professor of Ophthalmology and Neurobiology at the University of California, Davis, and chairman of the Department of Neurobiology, Physiology, and Behavior.

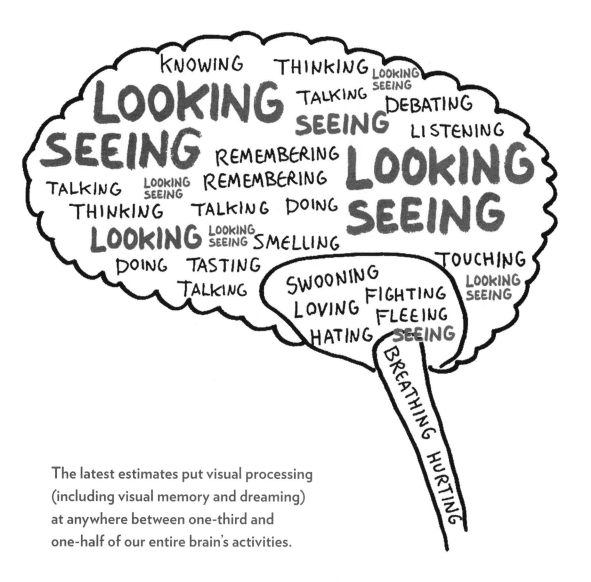

The latest estimates put visual processing (including visual memory and dreaming) at anywhere between one-third and one-half of our entire brain's activities.

We are essentially walking, talking, vision-processing machines.

For example, on a sunny afternoon, our eyes will process about 2×10^{18} photons of light. That's roughly twice the number of stars in our entire galaxy. And that's just one day. *What's truly crazy is how many of them we will remember.*

Our visual mind NEVER sleeps.

If our eyes don't have something interesting to look at, we will make stuff up.

Then again, if we do have something interesting to look at, our mind can stay focused   .

And what do we like to look at most of all?

My AUDIENCE

ABILITY

The EXPLANATION

Hum.

PICTURES

HURDLE

The PITCH

$E=mc^2$

Go back and take a quick look over all our sample presentations. What do we see? **Every single slide contains a picture . . .**

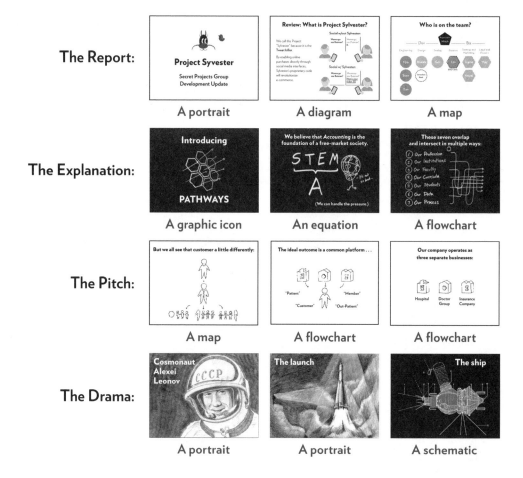

The Report:
- A portrait
- A diagram
- A map

The Explanation:
- A graphic icon
- An equation
- A flowchart

The Pitch:
- A map
- A flowchart
- A flowchart

The Drama:
- A portrait
- A portrait
- A schematic

A chart

A timeline

A flowchart

A portrait

A map

An equation

A map

A timeline

A flowchart

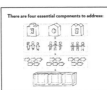

A flowchart

A flowchart

A portrait

A portrait

A portrait

A flowchart

A landscape

And every one of those pictures illustrates *one* of the six modes of thinking!

- **Who and what** are we talking about?
- **Where** are they located?
- **When** do they occur?
- **How much** is there?
- **How** do they interact?
- **Why** is this so?

It turns out that the six modes map *exactly* to how we see.

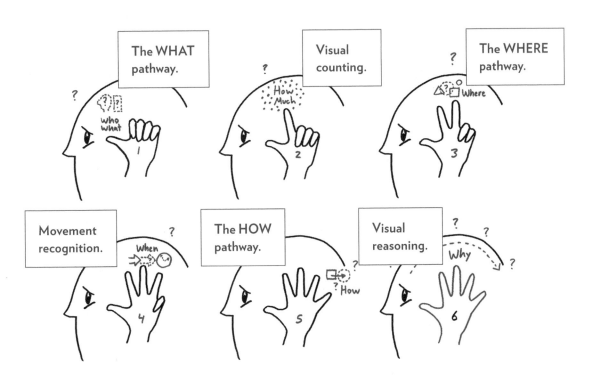

According to the latest insights in neurobiology, the primary "visual pathways" through which our eyes monitor the world align one to one to the six modes.

THIS MEANS SOMETHING POWERFUL.

IN ORDER TO ILLUSTRATE ANY STORY,
WE NEED ONLY SIX PICTURES:

WHO/ WHAT?

HOW MUCH?

WHERE?

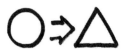

WHEN?

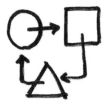

HOW?

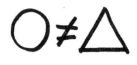

WHY?

With a little detail and style, we use these **six pictures** to show *anything* . . .

Portrait

Shows our players and objects.

Chart

Shows how much there is.

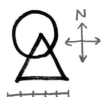

Map

Shows where they are located and overlap.

Timeline

Shows their sequence in time.

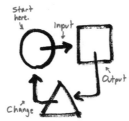

Flowchart

Shows the chains of cause, effect, and influence.

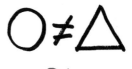

Equation

Shows the moral of the story.

We bring our storylines to visual life when we add two, three, four (or all six) of these pictures.

We bring all these storylines to life . . .

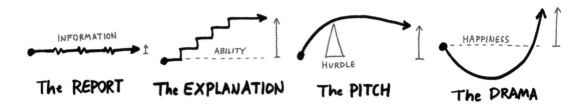

The REPORT   The EXPLANATION   The PITCH   The DRAMA

. . . by adding in combinations of these simple pictures:

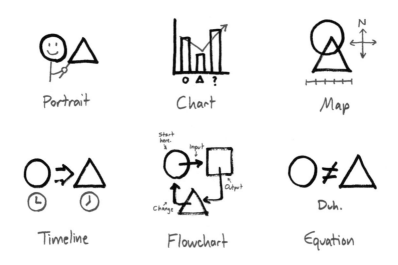

Portrait   Chart   Map

Timeline   Flowchart   Equation

To add pictures, we use this **picture pie** to simply translate what we SAY . . .

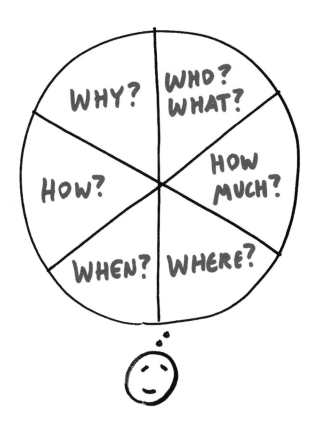

Using 6-Mode Thinking, we identify the essence of the main *verbal* ideas we've written down in our storyline . . .

. . . into what we **SHOW**.

. . . and then we translate those verbal ideas into their corresponding visual representations.

We typically start by drawing the main characters in our story (the "who and what") and then work our way around the **picture pie**, drawing as we go . . .

By the time we return to the top of the pie, we'll have every picture we need for our presentation.

Let's start at the top. When we describe **people**, **objects**, and **things**, we show a **portrait**.

"Balls"

Basketball   Baseball

rendering

"Your Friend"

Dark Hair
Blue
Flesh

portrait

Whos + Whats

"Birds"

plan

"My house"

elevation

Happy Person   Unhappy Person

Good Person   Bad Person

diagram

"PORTRAITS" = WHO AND WHAT?

During our presentation, when should we show a **PORTRAIT**?

1. Whenever we introduce a new character, group, or object.
2. Whenever that character appears again, especially in a different context. For example, a portrait appearing as part of a map.
3. When it is important to make each person or object distinct from all others.

How do we create a **PORTRAIT**?

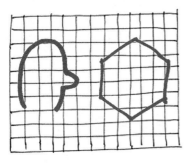

1. Think of most essential people and objects that appear in our presentation.
2. Write them down.
3. Find or draw the simplest possible picture that identifies each person or thing.
4. Do not worry about placement, overlap, or influence. (Those come later.)

When we describe **quantities**, **numbers**, and **values**, we show a chart.

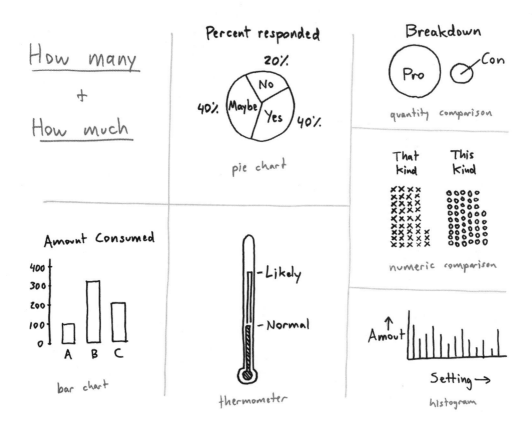

How many
+
How much

Percent responded

20%.

No

40%. Maybe Yes 40%.

pie chart

Breakdown

Pro   Con

quantity   comparison

That   This
kind   kind

XXXXX   ooooo
XXXXX   ooooo
XXXXX   ooooo
XXXXX   ooooo
XXXXX   ooooo
XXXXX   ooooo

numeric   comparison

Amount Consumed

400
300
200
100
0
    A   B   C

bar chart

- Likely

- Normal

thermometer

Amount ↑ ⊥ɪlıllıⅼ.lıⅼ

Setting →

histogram

"CHARTS" = HOW MUCH?

During our presentation, when should we show a **CHART**?

1. Whenever we introduce a measurement, a quantitative comparison, or a set of numeric data.
2. Whenever it is important that our audience see a measurable change or trend.
3. When we have quantitative evidence to share.
4. Whenever we wish to clarify or defuse an emotional argument.

How do we create a **CHART**?

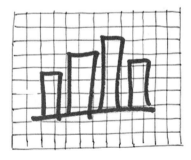

1. Identify our data set. (What are the things we are measuring?)
2. Create an *X* versus *Y* coordinate system upon which we can plot our numbers.
3. Map our data points onto the coordinates.
4. See if any interesting trends emerge.

When we describe **location**, **position**, and **overlap**, we show a map.

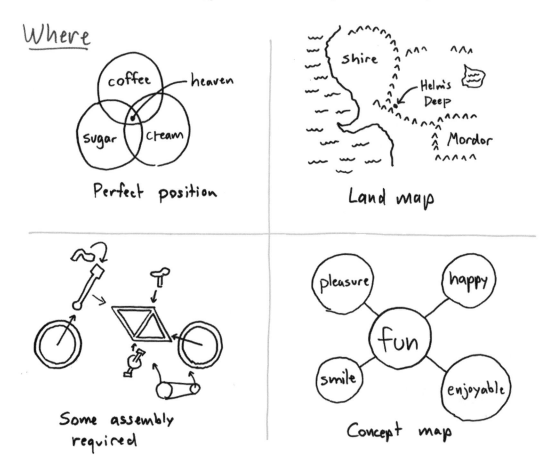

Where

coffee — heaven

sugar   cream

Perfect position

shire

Helm's Deep

Mordor

Land map

Some assembly required

pleasure   happy

fun

smile   enjoyable

Concept map

"MAPS" = WHERE ARE THINGS?

During our presentation, when should we show a **MAP**?

1. Whenever we wish to focus on the position of our characters and ideas relative to one another.
2. Whenever we want to show where we are.
3. Whenever we want to see the overlap between people, objects, or ideas.
4. Whenever we want to put a long list of people, items, or ideas into a more memorable context.

How do we create a **MAP**?

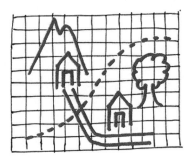

1. Identify our landscape (the places our characters or ideas are geographically or conceptually located) and the predominant features.
2. Create a north-south-east-west (or similar) coordinate grid.
3. Map the visible features onto the grid.
4. See if any interesting spatial relationships emerge.

When we describe **time**, **sequence**, and **order**, we show a timeline.

"TIMELINES" = WHEN DO EVENTS HAPPEN?

During our presentation, when should we show a **TIMELINE**?

1. Whenever we wish to focus on the position of our characters, ideas, and events in time.
2. Whenever we want to summarize a sequence.
3. Whenever we want to show the time dependencies between characters and their actions.
4. Whenever we want to put a long list of events into a broader context.

How do we create a **TIMELINE**?

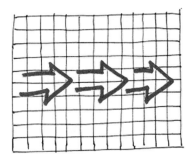

1. Identify our milestones. (What events take place during our sequence, plan, or idea?)
2. Create a **PAST › PRESENT › FUTURE** coordinate line.
3. Plot our milestones onto the line in sequential order, from beginning to end.
4. See if a realistic sequence emerges.

When we describe **cause and effect** or **process**, we show a flowchart.

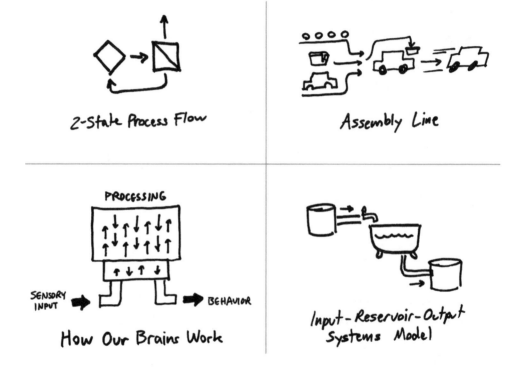

2-State Process Flow

Assembly Line

PROCESSING

SENSORY INPUT

BEHAVIOR

How Our Brains Work

Input-Reservoir-Output Systems Model

"FLOWCHARTS" = HOW DOES IT HAPPEN?

During our presentation, when should we show a **FLOWCHART**?

1. Whenever we wish to clarify cause and effect.
2. Whenever we want to understand the influence of one character or object upon another.
3. Whenever we want to see the flow of money, information, or influence.
4. Whenever we want to illustrate why something broke—or how to fix it.

How do we create a **FLOWCHART**?

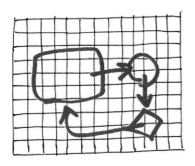

1. Identify the process we'd like to understand.
2. Draw the first step **HERE**.
3. Draw the final step **OVER THERE**.
4. Trigger by trigger, map in the decision or action points in between the first and final steps.
5. Review, test, revise.

When we describe the **moral of the story**, we show a visual equation.

Dogs love birds; birds don't love dogs.

$$\square + \triangle = \bigcirc$$

Object + Change = Different Object

Happy is better than sad.

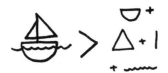

The whole is greater than the sum of its parts.

A bird in the hand...

"EQUATIONS" = WHAT IS THE LESSON?

During our presentation, when should we show an **EQUATION**?

1. Whenever we wish to convey the single most important insight or lesson from our entire presentation.
2. When we want to leave our audience with an indelible image of meaning.
3. Whenever we find ourselves tempted to say, "The moral of this story is _____."
4. When we want a laugh at the end of a long lesson.

How do we create an **EQUATION**?

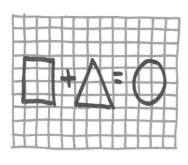

1. Review our entire thought process in creating all of the previous pictures.
2. Ask ourselves, "If I could help my audience remember just ONE THING . . . what would that thing be?"
3. Draw that lesson using PORTRAITS connected by mathematical symbols:
   -> + - = < >

Let me show you exactly what I mean.

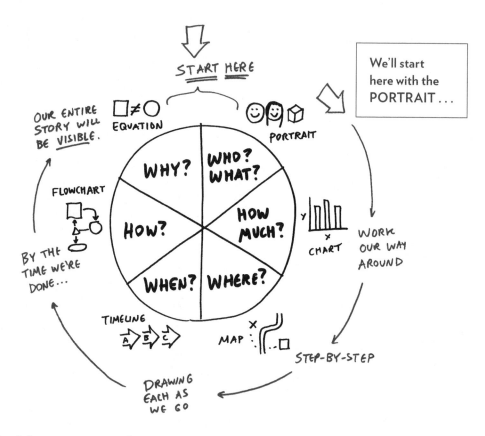

On the following pages, we're going to explain a complex process using nothing more than these six pictures, in clockwise order from the top.

CAN YOU EXPLAIN "CHESS" TO ME?

We could equally well illustrate other games like soccer or poker, or we could describe a business process, or we could map strategic decision making—or almost anything else—using the same six pictures.

Sure. Let's start with a **PORTRAIT** showing the **who** and the **what**.

Show:

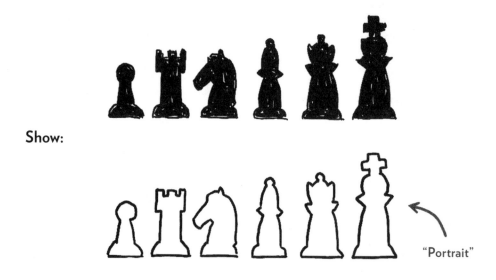

"Portrait"

Tell: In chess there are two teams. Each team has several different pieces, from a pawn to a king.

Next, let me show you **how many** there are and **how much** they are worth.

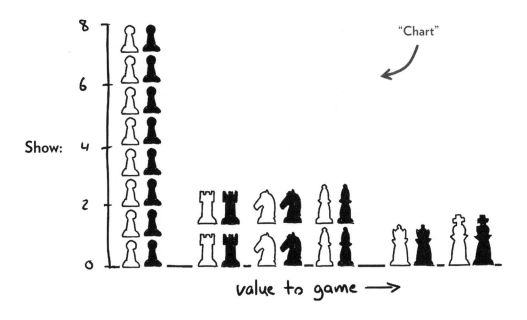

"Chart"

Show:

value to game →

Tell: This **CHART** shows us that there are lots of pawns, but they're not usually very valuable. Then again, there are only two queens, and they're really valuable.

This **MAP** shows **where** all the pieces sit at the beginning of the game.

Show:

"Map"

Tell: At the beginning of the game, all the black pieces sit in these squares, and all the white pieces in those squares.

When the game begins, we take turns moving the pieces.

"Timeline"

Show:

Tell: This **TIMELINE** shows a set of moves. First, you move your white pawn. Then I move my black pawn. Oops: You take my pawn with your bishop (and so on . . .).

We can show **how** the whole game plays out on this **FLOWCHART**.

Show:

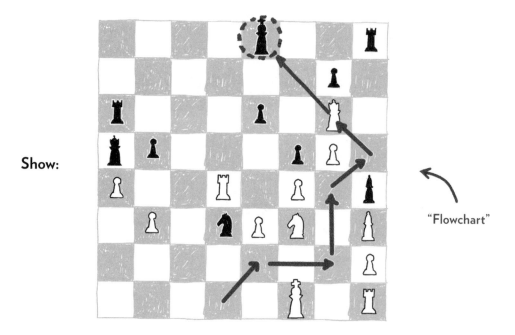

"Flowchart"

Tell: As the game goes on, we develop strategies as we see the cause and effect of different moves.

In the end, the **why** is revealed: The whole point is to take down each other's king.

"Equation"

Show:

Tell: This is what we call a VISUAL EQUATION. It's the moral of the story made visually clear and unforgettable.

Those were our **six pictures**.

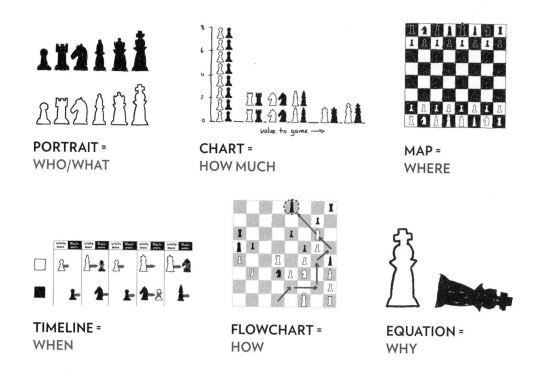

PORTRAIT =
WHO/WHAT

CHART =
HOW MUCH

MAP =
WHERE

TIMELINE =
WHEN

FLOWCHART =
HOW

EQUATION =
WHY

If we could so clearly map the essentials of chess with these pictures, what's to stop us from doing the same with any other idea?

In every presentation we use these same six pictures. **All that changes are the** DETAILS **and the** STYLE.

- **Details** = We use the **presentation pie** to tell us which picture to show. **Who and what** = **portrait**, **how much** = **chart**, and so on.

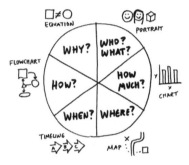

- **Style** = The only question that remains is whether we should we use photos, graphics, or drawings.

LET'S TALK PICTURE STYLE. WE HAVE THREE STYLES TO CHOOSE FROM:

PHOTOS ARE GOOD.

Pros:
- Easy to find. (Online image search is a gift from heaven.)
- No need to draw.
- Colorful and evocative.

Cons:
- Rarely show exactly what we want.
- Tend to be too specific.
- Challenging to edit.
- Lots of usage and copyright limitations.
- Can easily overshadow the speaker.

GRAPHICS ARE GREAT.

Pros:
- We can make custom graphics to show exactly what we want.
- Not too hard to create using the basic drawing tools in any presentation app.
- Relatively easy to keep simple.

Cons:
- Very easy to make too complex.
- Require some time to create well.
- Tend to be visually "cold"—which can be ideal for reports and pitches.

DRAWINGS ARE BEST.

Pros:
- With practice, these require very little time to create.
- Show exactly what we want.
- Are "warm" and inviting to look at.
- Show a human touch.
- Easy to keep simple.

Cons:
- Require basic drawing skills.
- Can become overly "cute"—which is mostly a problem in reports and pitches.

PHOTOS ARE EASY TO FIND AND USE.

They work well to support big ideas.

Because it has one clear center, **this** is a better presentation photo than **this**.

A simple photo is always best.
Make sure that your photo focuses on one big thing, and that thing is clear, centered, and obvious. Anything else becomes a visual distraction as our audience's eyes dart around searching for the message.

Landscape and still-life photos are great for evoking a mood.
Our audience wants to see US and OUR truth. Photos should evoke or support us. They are a backdrop to us, not the other way around. In most cases, the less specific the photo is, the more powerful.

BUT PHOTOS OF PEOPLE CAN REALLY MESS THINGS UP.

Who would you rather look at?

Them?

or

Me?

Which is reality? Them? or Me?

Overly beautiful stock photos actually damage our message. Our audience knows the picture isn't "true," and disconnects from us: *If we're lying about this, what else are we lying about?*

Unless we're referring to a specific person, avoid photos of actual people.
Real people are so evocative that they invariably distract from us and our message. Our audience's personal associations with known faces and features will overwhelm their ability to think about our message.

Avoid stock photography of people, period.
In advertising and Web sites, stock photos can trigger exactly the right response. But that is not true in a presentation. Why? Staged photos of people compete with the person actually on the stage. **If there is an emotion we want conveyed, we should find a way to convey it ourselves.**

SIMPLE **GRAPHICS** ARE GREAT.

They show exactly what we want and (with a little practice) are easy to create for all our picture types.

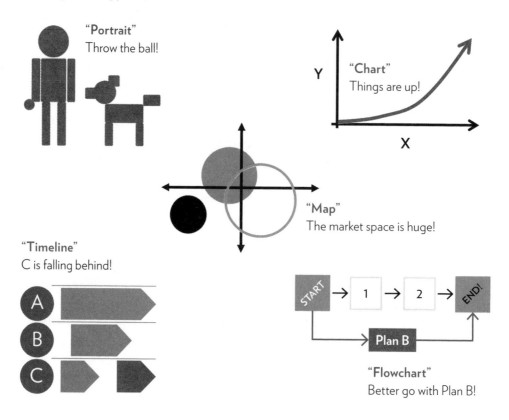

"Portrait"
Throw the ball!

"Chart"
Things are up!

"Map"
The market space is huge!

"Timeline"
C is falling behind!

"Flowchart"
Better go with Plan B!

With simple graphics, we can create every picture our presentation needs.

With a little practice, we can use even the simplest drawing tools to create captivating graphics. (This is especially helpful for people concerned about their hand drawing skills.)

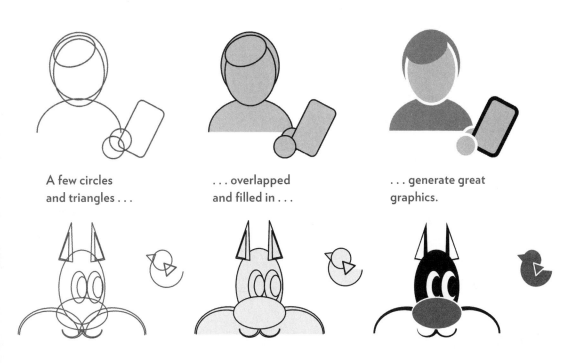

A few circles
and triangles . . .

. . . overlapped
and filled in . . .

. . . generate great
graphics.

In fact, every picture in the "Project Sylvester" report was created using only the tools in Microsoft PowerPoint.

But **drawing** is the best.
Here is how to do it.

All drawing starts with five simple shapes:

Can you draw these?

SQUARE　　CIRCLE　　TRIANGLE　　LINE　　BLOB

By combining them, we can draw nearly anything.

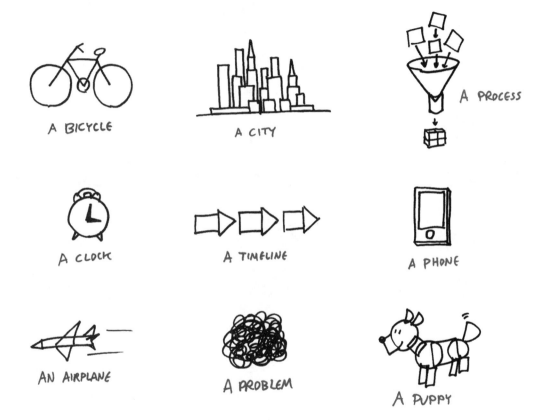

Every picture in the "health care" pitch was created using these kinds of basic shapes.

LET'S TALK FOR A MOMENT ABOUT DRAWING PEOPLE . . .

It's a surprise how easy it can be to draw people.

The trick is to keep things simple. Just use our basic lines and shapes.

Stick Figures = EMOTION

Yes!

FINE

OOPS.

ACK!

NOPE.

Sniff.

Hmm...

REALLY.

Simple stick figures are great for showing emotion. Just draw a head and a body and a couple arms and legs. Then add eyes and a mouth.

Block Figures = ACTION

Follow through...

Gone fishin'.

Working hard, or
hardly working?

Outta here!

Block figures are great for showing action. A box for the body, a circle for the head.
Attach a couple of lines, and with practice we've got life.

Blob Figures = RELATION

Halt. who goes there?

Kumbaya!

Outnumbered.

Little "blob" figures are best for images in which the individuals are less important than the relationships among groups.

THERE ARE TWO WAYS TO ADD DRAWINGS TO OUR PRESENTATION:

1. We draw sketches on paper and scan them in.

For quick visual storytelling, nothing is better than a pen and paper. We sketch our idea, redraw it once or twice, take a photo, and e-mail it to ourselves. Presto: instant presentation picture.

2. We draw directly on-screen.

Any tablet or pen-enabled laptop offers an excellent way to get our drawings into our presentations. Just draw, save, and insert.

Here's a neat trick of the trade: If we draw most of our picture in advance, and then touch it up live, our audience will be glued to the presentation.

Before the show, we draw *most* of our picture—but we leave a few details blank. (This works for computers, flip charts, and whiteboards.)

Then during the show, we draw the final pieces directly on-screen. Magic ensues.

Ooooh hhh!!

An amazing thing happens when we show the audience a mostly drawn picture and then quickly add in the final touches: Our audience believes we drew the entire picture in front of them. With practice, this is a powerful trick that can captivate and fascinate.

A QUICK Q&A ABOUT DRAWING . . .

Q: What if I can't draw?

A: I'm pretty sure you can. Remember: This isn't about drawing what we see *out there* in the world; it's about drawing what we see *in here* in our minds. Often that's nothing more than simple shapes.

Q: What if I've tried, and my drawings look terrible?

A: Practice. The first time you talked you didn't make any sense either—but it didn't take that long before you were pretty fluent.

Q: What if I really, really can't draw? (I mean *really*.)

A: You've still got great options: (1) Sit down with someone who can draw and describe to them your thinking, (2) Find simple images online and make sure you have permission to use them, (3) Use simple shapes within a basic presentation or word processing app, and (4) Create simple charts with a spreadsheet.

Q: How can I use technology to help me draw?

A: Nothing beats pen and paper, but hardware and software are getting pretty good now. Anything I say here will be out of date in a week, but remember this: It's not the computer that draws, it's us. Computers just make it less messy.

WHEN IT COMES TO PICTURES, REMEMBER THIS:

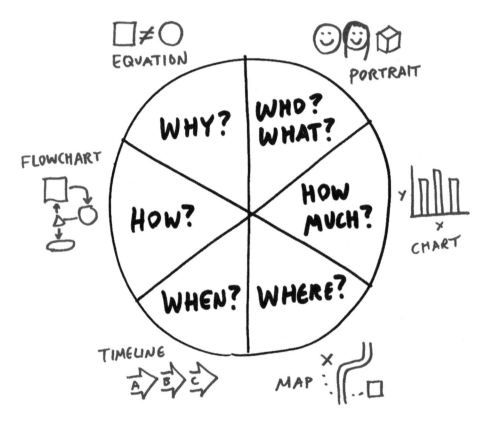

We ask ourselves, "What am I trying to say with this slide?" then beg, borrow, or create the corresponding picture.

A FINAL THOUGHT ABOUT PICTURES

Oh. Hello.

The ideal picture is as simple as a clear sentence. It enters our eye and tells a story. It doesn't call much attention to itself.

To help, we should limit detail, color, shading, and 3-D effects. These tend to draw attention to the picture rather than to the idea.

The ideal picture is just the essence of an idea made instantly visible, and nothing more.

CHAPTER 5

HOW NOT TO WORRY

FOR MOST OF US, GIVING A PRESENTATION IS LIKE GOING TO THE DENTIST.

We might not like it, but at some point we're going to have to do it.

As we move from preparation to presentation, we need to talk about the number one reason presenting is so hard:

FEAR.

The number one fear among Americans is public speaking. Which is totally understandable. **And totally fixable.**

PUBLIC SPEAKING IS A FUNNY THING.

Nothing is more important to our personal and professional success than being able to speak well in public. Yet for most of us, nothing is more terrifying.

The one thing we most need to do well is the one thing we're most afraid to do.

No wonder success is hard.

THE GOOD NEWS IS THAT WE ARE ALL
NATURAL-BORN PRESENTERS.

We were born knowing how to convey our idea to our audience.
(And at one point we were really good at it.)

As we grew up, some of us loved presenting and some of us hated it.

Either way, we had to do it.

As time goes on, our circumstances change, but the job remains the same.

Either way, we still have to do it.

NO MATTER WHERE WE FALL ALONG
THE STAGE-FRIGHT SPECTRUM, THERE IS HOPE:

Name:	**THE WORRIER**	**THE PANICKER**	**THE CAREFREE**
Symptoms:	We feel anxious when asked to give a presentation.	We feel anxious when we get onstage.	We don't have any anxiety about public speaking.
Incidence:	Common.	Universal.	Exceedingly rare.
What's at stake:	For most people, a manageable issue that resolves itself through planning. (If worry persists and grows over time, there is no shame in seeking professional help.)	Our body exhibits real (and scary) physiological symptoms of fear. Practice gives us the confidence to recognize and address these symptoms—and with time, to bypass them altogether.	What a great place to be! But there is a potential downside: If we become so cocky that we never prepare, we won't be ready for the unexpected. And in public speaking, the unexpected is guaranteed.
The best short-term fix:	Planning helps us settle our mind, exert control, and take effective action. (All of which help alleviate long-term worry.)	Practice helps alleviate real-time panic by giving us confidence in ourselves and our idea. Long term, practice makes us presentation pros.	We should be overjoyed with our luck. (Either that or we're lying.) Practice regardless.

WE CHANNEL FEAR AWAY BY KNOWING WHAT IT IS.

Anxiety is with us for a reason; it protects us from the unexpected. It reminds us to perform well when the stakes are high. We go wrong when we lose our sense of proportion and the anxiety becomes fear. Then it can eat us alive.

So rather than hiding it away, we're going to invite the anxiety in, understand how it can motivate us, and then channel the rest away.

ALTHOUGH **FEAR** IS REAL, IT ISN'T ALL A BAD THING.

Our most ancient mind says, "You're going to be in front of a lot of people who are going to judge you. Perform well or else!"

Our mind is telling us that we're about to do something risky—so we'd better be ready. If we take that as a gentle reminder to be prepared, we can learn to enjoy the risk.

Because on the flip side of **FEAR** is **FUN**.

WORRY DISSOLVES INSTANTLY ON CONTACT WITH PLANNING.

Sure, **planning** doesn't actually remove the physiological roots of worry, but it does replace the anxiety with meaningful action—and that's enough to get us going.

Here are five reliable steps to help us move beyond pre-presentation fear:

1. Get our presentation assignment. Start filling our buckets.
2. Select our storyline and organize it with the appropriate PUMA.
3. Refine the PUMA and add our pictures.
4. Do our plugs-out test. (See the next page.)
5. Do it again, only this time with our audience.

Guess what? We just gave an extraordinary presentation.

Now do you see why we filled up those buckets?

— Ready

FEAR FADES WITH **PRACTICE**.

Confidence comes from knowing our material through **practice**.
How do we practice? **Plugs out.**

"Plugs out" is what NASA calls the final test before a rocket launch. The test eliminates any question of "Can we do it in space?" by proving it with a "Yes" on the ground. We're going to do the same thing for the stage.

WHAT NOT TO DO

We do not sit in the back of the room, click through our slides, and say, "Here is where I'll talk about the technology, here is where I'll say blah blah . . ." We're not going to say that when we present, so we don't condition ourselves to say it when we practice. The plugs-out test works because it allows us no shortcuts.

If we do the plugs-out test right, the first time we will hate it. In fact, the plugs-out test is the hardest part of our entire presentation—even harder than our real talk. That's why we do it—and that's why we do it twice: because the second time we'll be relaxed enough to see and hear our presentation as our audience will.

How to Do the Plugs-Out Presentation Test:

1. Find a room that looks as close as possible to where we're going to be speaking.

2. Set up all our stage, audio, video, and technology as close as possible to the way it will be when we present.

3. Walk up onstage. Look at our missing audience.

4. Talk through our entire speech, word for word, picture for picture.

5. Repeat.

As we approach the stage, let's look back at what has brought us this far.

WE PREPARED AND PLANNED.

Why have we put so much focus on **truth**, **story**, and **pictures**? Because if we get those right, everything that follows will be a breeze. (Well, almost.)

WE PRACTICED.

It is absolutely true that if we practice well, our performance becomes easy.

So instead of worrying about what to say or how we look, we can focus on connecting with our audience.

NOW WE'RE READY TO PERFORM.

awesome.

PERFORM!

No matter how we've been anticipating it—with joy, excitement, or terror—the day of our performance will come. We *will* find ourselves on the stage, the audience *will* be there, and we *will* begin to **present**.

And you know what? When we trust our idea and are confident, we *will* enjoy our time onstage and we *will* help our audience change.

And that is what it's all about.

THE VIEW FROM THE FRONT

It is always a shock the first few times we suddenly realize all eyes are on us. Here is my list of favorite things to keep in mind when it's finally time to perform.

WARM UP THE ENGINE.

I want to thank you all for coming today...

The morning of our talk, the shower is our first audience. There is no better place on earth to recap our main points. Then as we head to the venue, we keep the engine warm by introducing ourselves to a few audience members. (This is the moment for which small talk was invented.)

From this point on, the waiting really is the hardest part. If we're in the audience, this is the perfect time to listen well to the other speakers. There's always something in their talk we can reflect on in ours. If we're stuck backstage, it's great to find someone to chat with. (If we're at a big production, remember that the roadies—who have seen it all—love to share a funny story.)

Then just before we go on, we say our opening line one more time—just to hear ourselves and know our engine is running.

SAND OUT THE BUMPS.

What's this BURR doing in my opening??

STORY BURR TALE ANECDOTE FACT

The most important part of any presentation is the first two minutes. That's when our audience decides who we are and how to listen to us, and that's the runway we use to get ourselves on a roll.

We should remove anything from the first few minutes of our presentation that trips us up. (We'll know that from our plugs-out test.) We always want to have our opening setup or story ready to go. With our opening nailed, we can start to relax for the rest of our talk.

And we **never, ever apologize** for any anxiety. Our audience doesn't know we're nervous, so why tell them? That'll just make them worry too. A far better way to let off that steam is to prepare a story in advance that's easy to tell and relaxes us; anything that makes us smile is guaranteed to make our audience smile.

SLOW IS BEAUTIFUL.

Who said speaking was hard?

Time travels differently onstage; we need to slow things down. What feels like a natural pace to us looks like a mad rush to our audience. We should often remind ourselves to take our time. (That doesn't mean say more; it means say less, and say it slower.) Nothing relaxes us more than taking a couple slow, deep breaths. (And everybody looks great in slow motion.)

That feels RIGHT!

FIND OUR OWN TRUE SWING.

Some of us are funny. Some of us are serious. Some of us are quick. Some of us are quiet. The truer we are to our own natural "stage" self, the more extraordinary our presentation. But until we've been up there a few times, our stage self may be a mystery. So we pick a pace and style and see how it feels. After just a few talks, we'll begin to find our own true swing.

FIND A FEW FRIENDS.

No matter how many people are in the room, we never really talk to all of them. We see a few friendly faces and just talk to them. If we look back to the same person three times, we can almost guarantee they will smile and nod—which gives us all a boost.

AND LAST OF ALL, LET'S NEVER FORGET THAT WE'VE GOT A LITTLE MAGIC ON OUR SIDE.

It is our natural human state to be curious; we are all hardwired to want to learn. Our trick as presenter is to trigger moments of discovery for our audience as often as we can. By varying our pace, keeping things visual, eliminating distractions, taming confusion, and never letting go of our storyline, we make our presentation feel like a bit of magic.

CHAPTER 6
THE GIFT

At any presentation, our audience is investing a part of their lives in us.

Let's give them a show.

In the end, presenting is a simple thing: We're just trying to get what is in our heads into our audience's heads as quickly, clearly, and believably as we can.

The best gift we can give ourselves is learning how to show and tell.

The best gift we can give one another is an extraordinary presentation.

Enjoy your idea.

Enjoy yourself.

Enjoy your audience.

This is going to be fun.

ACKNOWLEDGMENTS

Making this book simple was really hard—especially for the people who helped me. It is impossible to thank these friends enough for their support, insight, patience, and love. But let's try.

Isabelle Salvadori: For six trips through the drafts, from front to back, and for telling me so much with one look. Quote: "It will be brilliant if you cut out half."

Sophie Salvadori-Roam: For the stories and music. Quote: "I've been working on my story . . . and I have a new song."

Ted Weinstein: For the proposals, the negotiations, the contracts, the negotiations, the outlines, and the negotiations. Quote: "Breathe."

Dan Thomas: For the early morning phone brilliance that always made me think again. Quote: "Have you thought about . . ."

Jim Edwards: For the title. For the two pitches. For the obstacle course. Quote: "Just call it 'Show and Tell.' Jeez, dude, how hard is that?"

Lisa Solomon: For all the cheering all along the way. Quote: "Your ears must be burning . . ."

Xavier Fan: For endlessly supporting the technology of intuition. Quote: "I can't help it; I'm an engineer."

Emily Angell: For pulling it all together. Quote: "I managed to push back the deadline."

Eric Eislund: For your friendship. And the burritos. Quote: "Lunch?"

Daniel Lagin: For making it beautiful. Quote: "Yeah, I'm kinda done with the hand-drawn fonts myself."

Adrian Zackheim: For making it happen. Quote: "Where's my proposal?"

Tom Neilssen and **Les Tuerk**: For getting me onstage, again and again and again. Quote: "Can you be in Chicago on Thursday?"

Goh Ai Yat: For single-handedly supporting the eastern half of the globe. Quote: "Ready to Skype?"

Tim West: For proving that this can be taught. Quote: "Here's the rubric . . ."

Julie Smith David and **Tracey Sutherland**: For introducing a whole new world of unexpected visualizers. Quote: "Accountants really are fun, aren't they?"

Gary Roam: For demonstrating that show and tell can be life's greatest profession. (After flying, of course.) Quote: "Want to try that Cuban-Eight again?"

Nancy Beckman: For the sanity. Quote: "Don't rely on a broken gas gauge."

And to all my **Cadets** and **Associates** at **The Napkin Academy**: Thank you for staying with me through the whole dang thing. We did it!

Thank you.

FURTHER READING

ON STORYLINES THAT MATTER:

Joseph Campbell, *The Hero with a Thousand Faces*
Peter Guber, *Tell to Win*

Frank I. Luntz, *Words That Work*
Johan Sachs, *Winning the Story Wars*
Christopher Vogler, *The Writer's Journey*
Kurt Vonnegut, *A Man Without a Country*

ON PRESENTING LIKE WE MEAN IT:

Cara Hale Alter, *The Credibility Code*
Nancy Duarte, *slide:ology* and *resonate*

Carmine Gallo, *The Presentation Secrets of Steve Jobs* and *Talk Like TED*
Garr Reynolds, *Presentation Zen*

ON MAKING PICTURES AND CREATING VISUAL GOODNESS:

Sunni Brown, *The Doodle Revolution*
Alicia Diane Durand, *Discovery Doodles*
Ed Emberley, *Make a World*

David and Tom Kelley, *Creative Confidence*
Austin Kleon, *Steal Like an Artist*

ON NOT WORRYING TOO MUCH:

Susan Cain, *Quiet*
Mihaly Csikszentmihalyi, *Flow: The Psychology of Optimal Experience*

Daniel Kahneman, *Thinking, Fast and Slow*
Daniel Pink, *Whole New Mind*

SUPPORTING VIDEOS TO WATCH:

TED Talks: Hans Rosling (YouTube: Jan. 16, 2007)
TED Talks: Jill Bolte Taylor (YouTube: Mar. 13, 2008)

Kurt Vonnegut, *On the Shapes of Stories* (YouTube: Oct. 30, 2010)

On the shoulders of giants